INSIDE ISLAM

Exposing and Reaching the World of Islam

REZA F. SAFA

Charisma®
HOUSE
Books about Spirit-Led Living

INSIDE ISLAM by Reza F. Safa
Published by Charisma House
A part of Strang Communications Company
600 Rinehart Road
Lake Mary, FL 32746
www.charismahouse.com

Library of Congress Catalog Card Number: 95-74817
International Standard Book Number: 0-88419-416-7

01 02 03 04 05   11 10 9 8 7
Printed in the United States of America

This book is dedicated to all of our faithful partners throughout the world. Your support and prayers have made it possible for us to reach multitudes of unreached people with the gospel of Jesus Christ. Thanks for being the backbone of this ministry. With your continued help we will reach millions of people for Jesus.

ACKNOWLEDGMENTS

First of all, I would like to thank my beloved wife, Marilyn. You are the joy of my heart and a true partner and friend. Thank you for being patient with me.

I am grateful to Jim Olson and John Mason. Thank you for giving me a chance and believing Jesus in me.

Thank you to Deborah Poulalion and the editors from Charisma House for your tremendous editing work on this book.

Thanks also to Carl Ellis for your contribution of the statistics on African American converts to Islam.

Thanks to Kaveh, Christopher, Tallat and Faheemah for allowing me to record your testimonies in this book.

I would like to thank Virginia Prochnow and again my wife, Marilyn, for your proofreading.

Last and above all I want to thank my beloved Lord and Savior, Jesus Christ, without whom I would still be bound in the chains and shackles of a dark religion.

CONTENTS

I will say to the north, "Give them up!"
And to the south, "Do not keep
them back!"
Bring My sons from afar,
And My daughters from the ends
of the earth —
Everyone who is called by My name,
Whom I have created for My glory;
I have formed him, yes,
I have made him.
Isaiah 43:6-7

ISLAM — A WORLD POWER

ON TUESDAY, SEPTEMBER 11, 2001, America's soul was scarred by a great and unprecedented tragedy. A group of Muslim fundamentalists hijacked four passenger aircrafts and used them as weapons of mass destruction. They brought down the World Trade Center Twin Towers in New York City and crashed into the Pentagon in Washington, D. C. Why would a group of religious people do that to innocent people? What is their motive? Why do they hate us so dreadfully that they are willing to kill themselves and thousands of innocent people? Where does that hate come from? How can they murder so mercilessly and ruthlessly? Why do they hate American government and American people?

To understand the answers to the above questions, one must understand the spirit under which these men operate — the spirit of Islam. What is Islam? What does Islam want? Where is Islam going? What is Islam requiring from its adherents? Are these terrorists ordinary Muslims? Why are some Muslims more violent than others?

This book presents a view of Islam that may be contrary to what you have heard from other sources. To understand, we must take a look at our changing, transitioning world over the past few decades.

The eighties and nineties were decades of transition and enormous change, both in the natural and the spiritual realms. They were a period of shifting — politically, economically and spiritually from one era to another. The world passed from the cold war era of communism to an age of new threats by the Islamic fundamentalists; from dealing with atheists to an increased concern with religious extremists. The political map of the world took a new shape, and new unpredicted boundaries were drawn.

The political and economic highlight of this period was the bankruptcy and fall of the Soviet Union and its Eastern European allies. The walls of an antichrist empire came tumbling down, an oppressive empire which had suppressed the truth and freedom for several decades.

Communism was a system of religious beliefs. Even though the bylaws of that system did not include the Ten Commandments or the worship of the one true God, its heroes, Marx and Lenin, were adored as divine and followed as gods. In the pursuit and spread of their ideology, communists were as fanatical as some religious people.

With the fall of communism, the world was ready to embrace another antichrist force, a spiritual principality that would resist and oppose freedom and truth. This force, however, would be covered with a religious outfit and would possess a greater authority over the lives and minds of its followers than communism ever did. This power which would soon become a threat to world peace was a spiritual force called Islam.

Islam is a world religion with more than one billion adherents — one out of five people in the world are Muslims. Islam dominates in many political and social arenas and in multitudes of cultures and people groups. It reigns in more than forty-five Muslim nations, and its roots have reached almost every possible corner of this earth. It is a world power spiced with many cultures.

Islam in Africa is not the same as Islam in the Middle East or Islam in India. Consequently Muslims differ one from another in their beliefs, practices and behaviors. However, they all have one thing in common — Allah is their God, and Muhammad is their holy prophet.

To the Western mind, Islam is an irrational and illogical sort of belief. Here in America, where most people have very little knowledge of this religion, Muslims are perceived as hostile, violent and anti-American religious people. The purpose of this book is not to analyze Islam in light of the political upheaval in the Middle East in the past decade. Nor will I lynch Islam because of the recent violent acts of Muslim fundamentalist groups, even though I will walk you through this past decade of events that have brought worldwide attention to Islam. My goal is to scrutinize Islam, its makeup and its history under the light of the gospel and allow readers to perceive for themselves the true nature of this religion.

By no means will I allow any spiteful or resentful attitudes toward Muslims to be concluded out of my writings. We must not judge all Muslims in the light of recent violence done by a small core of Muslim fundamentalists. It would be unjust and untruthful to do so. The core of Muslim extremists who abide by the fundamentals of Islam do not make up a sizable percentage of those who call themselves Muslims. As a matter of fact, Muslims in general are very loving and hospitable people.

We must probe Islam with spiritual discernment and not with any preconceived emotional or logical notions. If we fail to gain a spiritual understanding, the whole point and purpose of this book will have been missed.

I have read many books written by Western scholars, research writers and Islamic apologetics whizzes. They have analyzed the history and the philosophy of Islam well, but they have missed the *spirit* of Islam.

This book will help you to understand the spirit of Islam. I will tell the history of the religion from an insider's point of view. I will also compare portions of the Koran to the Bible, revealing Satan's tactics of spiritual deception. I feel it is essential for Christians to understand some of the religious teaching that Muslims receive.

For American readers, I have included a special chapter on the Black Muslim movement in America. I also discuss the Nation of Islam, the most visible Black Muslim group, led by Louis Farrakhan.

Because the church has failed to understand Islam, the Islamic people have not been stirred or touched by the gospel of Jesus Christ. They remain in the darkness of a fanatical religion which forces them to have faith in a god who is unreachable, untouchable and unknowable.

I was a fanatical Muslim myself, and I know of many Muslims who truly hunger for the truth of God. They do not know Jesus because they have not heard of Him. I pray that this book will open your eyes to notice the Muslims in your community who need the hope that Christianity can give them for forgiveness of sins and peace with God. I want this book to prepare you to become a part of the great challenge of reaching the Muslim world for God. May the Lord burden you with love and compassion for this vast harvest of unreached souls.

PART I

WHAT IS ISLAM?

ONE

THE SPIRIT OF ISLAM

THE SPIRIT OF ISLAM IS rising up throughout the world. Islam is beginning to retrieve its former status as a world power, a power which appropriates new territories by force, fear, war and bloodshed.

Since 1979 the world has witnessed the unprecedented violence of terrorist activities committed by Muslim fundamentalists throughout North Africa and the Middle East. The West, especially the United States, has been the prime target of the hatred and violence of these Muslim fundamentalist groups.

In 1979 a group of Muslim students seized the U.S. Embassy in Tehran and held fifty-two Americans hostage for 444 days. That same year the U.S. Embassy in Islamabad,

Pakistan, was set on fire by a group of Muslim fundamentalists. In 1982 thirty-seven Americans and other Westerners were taken hostage by Hezbollah in Lebanon. The last American was freed in 1991. In 1983 Hezbollah conducted three suicide bomb attacks in Beirut — at the American Embassy and the United States and French military barracks — killing 350 people, including 241 U.S. Marines. In 1985 Hezbollah struck again by hijacking a TWA jetliner to Beirut, killing a U.S. Navy diver on board. In 1988 another Islamic group was responsible for a Pan Am jetliner being blown up in the air over Scotland, killing all 259 passengers on board.

During the 1980s nearly one hundred foreigners were kidnapped in Lebanon by the Hezbollah. At least eight of these hostages were killed, including three Americans.

Even more recently, in February 1993, a powerful bomb rocked the World Trade Center in New York City, killing six people and injuring at least one thousand. Sheik Omar Abdel Rahman and fourteen of his followers were arrested and charged with the bombing. *Time* magazine reported that Abdel Rahman is the spiritual leader to groups that allegedly plotted to blow up a federal building in Manhattan, the United Nations building, the Lincoln and Holland Tunnels, and the George Washington Bridge.[1]

Abdel Rahman and his followers were indicted with several serious allegations of terrorist activities. The indictment said they "unlawfully, willfully and knowingly combined, conspired, confederated and agreed together and with each other to levy a war of urban terrorism against the United States."[2]

Had these alleged plots been carried out, they would have caused untold death and destruction. The chaos and national sorrow would have been much greater than that caused by the Oklahoma City bombing in April 1995.

During the past three decades Islam has been in the

headlines throughout the world. The terrorist activities wrought by the Muslim fundamentalists along with other major events within the Islamic community, such as the Iranian revolution of Ayatollah Khomeini, the assassination of Egypt's President Anwar Sadat, the invasion of Kuwait by Saddam Hussein and the resulting Gulf War, have caused much concern in the Western hemisphere, especially here in the United States.

Khomeini's bitter political stand against the United States and its Western allies brought the hope of revolution to many fanatical Muslims who felt they were oppressed by Iran's pro-Western secular government. His Islamic revolution and his uncompromising fundamentalist leadership stirred the hearts of millions of Muslims around the world and aroused a new sense of boldness in Muslim communities. Khomeini became a hero of radical Muslims throughout the world. The former Algerian president Ahmed Ben Bella declared, "A brilliant light appeared in Iran which illuminated the whole Muslim world."[3]

A Sunni Muslim who is a cabinet minister in one of the Persian Gulf nations said in an interview in 1984, "There is a halo of respect for the thirty years of Mohammed and the first caliphs, their lives of devotion and poverty, living in humility and away from materialism, demonstrating a willingness to die [for the faith]. When Khomeini emerged, he symbolized all those things. He was worshiped by the Arabs and all the Islamic world. He was a source of inspiration for all. He captured the admiration of all."[4]

In Iran, Khomeini was considered an exceptionally holy man appointed and sent by Allah. They called him *Ruhollah* (*"rohe Allah"*), meaning the "spirit of Allah." Six months after returning to Iran from fifteen years in exile Khomeini declared, "The governments of the world should know that Islam cannot be defeated. Islam will be victorious in all the countries of the world, and Islam and the teachings of the Koran will prevail all over the world."[5]

To take Khomeini's declaration lightly is to be ignorant of the history of Islam and its accomplishments. We must realize that Islam has been, and today is, a potent political and economic force in the world.

In 1984 Dr. Marvin Zonis, director of the Middle East Institute at the University of Chicago, said:

> The message from Iran — no matter how bizarre or trivial it sounds on first, second, fourth or thirty-ninth hearing — is in my opinion the single most impressive political ideology which has been proposed in the 20th century since the Bolshevik Revolution...If we accept that Bolshevism is a remnant of the nineteenth century, then I want to argue that we've had only one good one in the 20th — and it's this one. This powerful message will be with us for a very long time — no matter what happens to Ayatollah Khomeini.[6]

The False Religion

Since Satan does not have any authority and power to stop us in the spiritual realm, he must find other ways to stop us. One way for him to hinder the advance of the kingdom of God on earth is to raise a physical force — another human being who has a strong will and determination.

Satan wants to disseminate his plans and ideas among humans and entice them to follow him radically. If Satan also gives these human beings social, political or religious status, they will become vessels for him to use against the church and the plan of God.

False religion is the greatest opposition that Satan has raised against God. From the time of the garden of Eden until this day, false religion has been Satan's paramount strategy for coming against the plan of God for mankind.

The spirit that was upon Cain was a religious spirit, a Pharisee spirit. Cain prepared an offering to God, but it was of no value because it wasn't the kind of offering God would accept. His offering was more of a religious ritual than an act of faith and love toward God. Abel, on the other hand, was counted righteous because God accepted his offering. Abel offered to God an offering by faith. Cain's heart was not right with God, so he hated his brother for being accepted by God. Thus, Cain was filled with rage and hatred, and he rose against his brother and killed him (see Gen. 4).

Cain's spirit is the kind of spirit that Satan uses to come against the righteous man. This kind of religious spirit is an open door for demonic influence. This religious spirit is hateful, vengeful, murderous and bloodthirsty. It is resentful, unforgiving and does not know mercy.

The Pharisees and Sadducees of Jesus' time had a religious spirit, and they persecuted Christians in the name of God. The complex system of teaching that they used to keep people in bondage constituted a false religion. Throughout history, false religions have been accompanied by the fruits of a religious spirit.

Test the Spirits

Every revelation received by man throughout history has come from one of three different sources — God's Spirit, the human spirit or a demonic spirit.

The Bible says, "Do not believe every spirit, but test the spirits, whether they are of God; because many false prophets have gone out into the world" (1 John 4:1). A condition is then given by which these spirits should be judged:

By this you know the Spirit of God: Every spirit

that confesses that Jesus Christ has come in the flesh is of God, and every spirit that does not confess that Jesus Christ has come in the flesh is not of God. And this is the spirit of the Antichrist, which you have heard was coming, and is now already in the world (vv. 2-3).

An antichrist spirit is a spirit that opposes the work and person of Christ. An antichrist spirit denies the deity of Jesus. It denies and despises the cross. It denies redemption and forgiveness through the shed blood of Jesus. It denies the death and resurrection of Jesus.

I am not talking about the Antichrist, the person who will be manifested before the return of Christ. I am speaking of the spirit of antichrist. John says, "Test the spirits." *Spirits* is plural, meaning there is more than one antichrist spirit. These are, of course, the demonic spirits who are fallen beings.

An antichrist spirit works mainly through false prophets. John acknowledges that "many false prophets have gone out into the world." I believe that every person who calls himself a prophet must be tested. The Bible says, "Let two or three prophets speak, and let the others judge" (1 Cor. 14:29). We must judge every revelation according to the Word of God. If the revelation does not align itself with the Word of God, it is not from God, no matter how it was given. I don't care if a host of angels came and manifested themselves and brought that revelation. The Bible warns us that Satan can appear as an angel of light (2 Cor. 11:14).

Islam denies the deity, death and resurrection of Jesus; therefore, it is an antichrist religion. Islam denies the shed blood of Jesus, and the redemption and forgiveness of sins through that blood; that makes Muhammad a false prophet and Islam a false religion.

In addition, Islam contradicts many facts and truths of the

Bible. The Koran gives numerous revelations that totally contradict the Bible and the God of the Bible. Islam also produces a religious spirit in its followers that results in violence, bloodshed and vengeance (just as it did with Cain and with the Pharisees).

We will carefully study the formation and the beliefs of Islam. As we do, you will see the nature, the goal and the purpose of this religion. The spirit that raised Islam has three main objectives:

1. To challenge Christ, His Word and His church

2. To hinder the end-time world revival

3. To oppose the Jewish people and take over their God-given land

I believe Islam is Satan's weapon to oppose God, His plan and His people. Let's look at the philosophy of Islam and see what Islam is really all about.

What Is Islam?

Islam is a very complicated and complex religion, far from any Judeo-Christian understanding.

Many political analysts, scholars and journalists have made untiring efforts to define and analyze Islam. Much research has been done, many interviews have been recorded and many books have been written; yet Islam remains an obscure, obtuse, irrational sort of ideology to the mind and culture of Western society.

To a Muslim, Islam is a complete system that encompasses every aspect of society. The Muslims assert that the laws of Islam meet not only the religious and the moral codes of a society, but the political, economical and ethical codes as well.

We must realize that many of the teachings of Islam are a

reflection of Arabian culture and society of the seventh century. Many rituals and practices enforced by Islam can be traced back to pre-Islamic Arabia. One researcher points out, "Archeological and linguistic work done since the latter part of the nineteenth century has unearthed overwhelming evidence that Muhammad constructed his religion and the Koran from pre-existing material in Arabian culture."[7]

Islam may be viewed as a revolutionary ideology against oppression, a religion enforcing ethical and moral laws or a political system different from those of capitalistic or socialistic origin. In my opinion, however, Islam is a spiritual force, an antichrist spirit manifested to oppose the work and the plan of God.

A Religion of Total Submission

The word *Islam* means "submission to Allah," and a Muslim is the one who submits to Islam. Submission is a strong characteristic of this religion. A Muslim must exhibit total surrender to Allah, a god who is absolute in everything and totalitarian in his ways of converting and subjecting his creations.

Allah demands total subjection of a person in all aspects of life. A tribe in seventh century Arabia acknowledged to Muhammad their faith in Allah by saying, "We believe in Allah!" Muhammad responded, "You have not believed until you say, 'We have submitted ourselves!'" (Sura 49:14).

To become a Muslim is to become the slave of Allah. Many Muslims are called *Abd-Allah,* meaning "a slave of Allah."

The goal of Islam is to produce a theocracy with Allah as the ruler of society, a society with no separation between religion and the state. This society would have no democracy, no free will and no freedom of expression.

In Islamic countries, opposition against Islam or against those who are believed to be appointed by Allah is not allowed. In a country like Iran, opposing a man like Ayatollah ("the sign of Allah") Khomeini is almost as severe as opposing Allah. Shiites, for instance, believe that Khomeini was appointed by Allah. The punishment for such an act in Iran is death.

When Islam takes over a home, family, society or country, it controls everything. This fact is observable in Islamic states. In Iran, for example, once the Islamic revolution took place and Khomeini became the leader, every aspect of that society became subject to the laws of Islam. Khomeini was regarded not only as a political or religious leader, but also as the builder of a new society totally devoted to Islamic laws and to the teachings and lifestyle of Muhammad.

The Islamic revolution of Ayatollah pierced through every part of Iranian society and changed almost everybody and everything in that nation — the ethical, moral, social behavior as well as the economic and political system. At the proclamation of the Islamic Republic of Iran on April 1, 1979, Khomeini said, "On this blessed day, the day the Islamic community assumes leadership, the day of victory and triumph of our people, I declare the Islamic Republic of Iran, the first day of God's government."[8]

In the West, religion is not allowed to have control and power over all phases of a society. Christians in neither Europe nor America can pronounce an obligatory law concerning the moral, ethical and social behavior of the citizens of their country. They may try to influence their society and the law of their country according to a biblical model, but they cannot enforce an ethical or moral law.

In an Islamic country, though, there is no separation between state and religion. The laws of Islam are the laws of the country. A citizen has no choice. Resisting these laws results in severe punishment.

The Foundation of Islam

Islam emanates from two fundamental sources, the Koran and the traditions of Muhammad (*hadith*). To the radical and fundamentalist Muslims, Islam is a comprehensive, self-evolving system. It is the ultimate path of life, an ideology or system able to govern every political, economic, social and cultural aspect of their society, applicable to all times and places.

Islam to a Muslim is more than a religion, more than daily rituals. Islam is a way of living, thinking and reasoning.

Knowing this will help you understand why Muslims think and reason so unlike people in Western societies. Islam obliges its followers to follow Muhammad's way of thinking. The first confession of Koran, the holy book of Muslims, is *"La Elahe al Allah"* and *"Muhammad an Rasoul al Allah,"* meaning "There is no God except Allah" and "Muhammad is his prophet." In the light of history, a more accurate interpretation would be: "There is no God who is allowed to be worshiped except Allah, and every man must follow Muhammad and his teachings."

In the Islamic nations, other religions do not have the right to exist. The few people who practice other religions are under tremendous oppression. They are routinely incarcerated and executed. An example of such execution was the murder of a key denominational leader in Iran in January 1994.

The Baal Cults

In order to understand the nature and character of Islam, one must look at Islam from a biblical point of view. Otherwise Islam remains an enigma, an unsolved puzzle. We need to explore the similarities between the Baal cults of the Old Testament and modern Islam.

In the Old Testament, the followers of Baal were major opposers and challengers of Jehovah God and His people. Baal, meaning "master," "possessor" or "husband," was worshiped as a male god of the Phoenicians and Canaanites. The worship of Baal was often connected with the goddess Ashtoreth (Judg. 2:13), the female counterpart. Baal was considered the sun god.

Baal worship not only involved lascivious practices of fertility cults (Num. 25:1-5), but even such abominations as child sacrifice (Jer. 19:5). Baal worshipers also ate sacrifices made to the dead (Ps. 106:28) and cut themselves with knives and lances (1 Kin. 18:28).

Jezebel, Ahab's wife, the daughter of Ethbaal ("with Baal"), who was king of the Sidonians, was a devout worshiper and prophetess of Baal who revived Baal worship in Israel. She furiously opposed Jehovah and His anointed prophets. She massacred many prophets of God (1 Kin. 18:4) and also created an atmosphere of fear throughout Israel to such an extent that even Elijah feared for his life and ran from her (1 Kin. 19:2-3).

Characteristics of Baal worship can be seen in many of today's cults and false religions. Baal worship produces a spirit of hatred towards God's elect, a spirit of immorality, fear, bloodshed, division and war.

Throughout history Islam has proved to have a similar nature and character. Many rituals practiced within Islam are similar to those of Baal worship. In my opinion, the spirit that raised Baal worship in Phoenicia and Canaan, and later in Babylon, is the same spirit that raised Islam in Arabia.

According to the *Encyclopedia of Religion, Allah* is a pre-Islamic name corresponding to the Babylonian *Bel* (Baal).[9] According to Middle East scholar E. M. Wherry, in pre-Islamic times both Allah-worship and Baal-worship of Baal involved the worship of the sun, the moon and the stars, which defines them as astral religions.[10] The crescent moon, which was the symbol of moon worship, is also the symbol of Islam. It is printed on the flags of many Islamic countries and placed on top of minarets and mosques.

Many Muslims will argue that Allah is the same God that Christians and Jews worship. But by studying the Koran one will see the vast gap of character, nature and personality that exists between the God of the Bible and the Allah of the Koran. It is not even necessary to be a Christian to see the immense differences — Muslims will see the difference if they study both the Koran and the Bible. Pointing out the differences would be a waste of time and energy. I will not commit the treason of comparing Jesus with any other man or comparing Christianity with any other philosophy that has ever existed upon the face of this earth. Jesus is far above every name that is ever mentioned or will ever be named.

All I need to do is to show honestly what Islam teaches and practices. Then you will know what Islam is. Jesus said, "A tree is known by its fruit" (Matt. 12:33). A banana tree produces bananas, and a thorn bush produces thorns. The fruit that Islam has produced throughout history will show its nature.

As we will see, the fruits of fear, terror and bloodshed have always characterized this religion. Let's examine the history of Islam and discover this for ourselves.

TWO

MUHAMMAD AND THE ORIGIN OF ISLAM

I N THE YEAR A.D. 570, Muhammad (meaning "praised") was born in the city of Mecca in Arabia. Muhammad's father, Abdollah ("slave of Allah*"), died before the birth of his son. Muhammad's mother, Amina, died when he was six years old. He was placed in the care of his grandfather, Abdol Mottaleb, who also soon died. Muhammad was then taken by his uncle, Abu Talib. Muhammad's family was a part of a very powerful tribe called Quraish.

At age twenty-five Muhammad married a wealthy widow named Khadijeh who was forty years of age. Khadijeh lived in Mecca, and through her Muhammad was introduced to

---

* Allah was one of the gods worshiped in Mecca even before Muhammad's rise to power.

the influential people in the Meccan society. Muhammad associated with the chief people of Mecca and became acquainted with the religious and political situation of his country.

In Arabia, people worshiped a number of deities. Mecca was a shrine city where the Ka'aba ("Cube") was located, a cubical building known as the "house of Allah." Muslims believe that this house was built by Abraham and his son Ishmael. Ka'aba was full of the images of other gods and goddesses. It was a custom of pilgrims who came to Mecca to walk around Ka'aba seven times, kissing and touching the Black Stone. The Black Stone was a meteorite to which great religious significance was attached. This pagan custom was later adopted by Muhammad in the Islamic pilgrimage of *hajj*.

Even though in the time of Muhammad there were both Christians and Jews in Arabia, it seems as though they lacked the power to convince the Arabs of the one, true God of the Bible.

Muhammad and other seekers of God used to go from time to time to a cave in the side of Mount Hira, some three miles north of Mecca, to meditate. Around the year 610 when Muhammad was forty years old, he had a visitation from an angel, whom Muhammad believed to be the angel Gabriel. The angel told him to recite. When Muhammad asked what he was to recite, the angel replied, "Recite, in the name of the Lord who has created, created man from the clots of blood. Recite, seeing that the Lord is the most generous, who has taught by the pen, taught man what he did not know" (Sura 96:1-5).

This experience brought a great doubt to Muhammad. Could this be a message from Allah, the God whom Arabs recognized to be the supreme God? No prophets had ever been sent to the Arabs. Muhammad shared the experience with his wife, and she assured him that he was appointed a prophet, a *rasoul* ("apostle") to the people.

For some months, during which time no more revelations came to Muhammad, he was deeply depressed and even considered suicide. After two years other revelations began to come to Muhammad in various forms. Sometimes he saw an angel; sometimes he only heard a voice, and sometimes a message came in a dream. When a revelation came to him, he would fall to the ground and foam at the mouth. The message came to him in the Arabic language, and Muhammad spoke the words that he received. These were then written down by those who heard him.

Muslims believe that Muhammad was illiterate. Therefore, Muslims believe that these revelations, which later on were collected by his followers in a book called Koran (which means "reciting" or "reading"), were not Muhammad's words but the very words of God. Thus, Muslims believe that the Koran is a miracle from God because an illiterate man could not write such a book. Over a period of twenty-two years these messages came to Muhammad on different occasions.

Soon Muhammad began to preach that there is no God but Allah, and that he was the prophet of Allah. He called upon people to repent from worshiping other gods and to turn to Allah. His first followers were from his family: Khadijeh, his wife; his adopted son Zaid; and a young cousin Ali. Later about one hundred more people, mainly people of humble origin, also joined the movement. Soon persecution from the leading people of the city began as Muhammad attacked the gods in the Ka'aba. The opposition was bitter, but they could not do anything to Muhammad because he was protected by his uncle Abu Talib.

At the end of the year 620, Muhammad suffered the losses of his wife, Khadijeh, and his uncle Abu Talib. A few months after the death of Khadijeh, Muhammad married the widow of one of the believers. He also married Ayisha, the seven-year-old daughter of his friend Abu Bakr.

Hijra — Muhammad's Migration to Medina

Unable to make any progress in Mecca, Muhammad decided to move to Yathrib, a city 280 miles north of Mecca, later to be known as Medina ("city of the Prophet"). This migration, called *Hijra* in Arabic, started on September 24, 622. This marks the beginning of Islam, and the Muslim calendar starts with this date.

During the second year in Medina, life became financially difficult for the followers of Muhammad. At this time the revelation came to Muhammad: "O Prophet, strive hard against unbelievers and be firm against them" (Sura 9:73).

With divine approval Muhammad started to raid the caravans of his enemies. The first raid was carried out successfully. This victory led Muhammad to attempt to capture a larger caravan. With 350 of his armed men, Muhammad attacked a caravan carrying much merchandise at a place called Badr, defeating an army of one thousand men who had come from Mecca to protect the caravan. The spoils were divided among Muhammad's men, and he kept one-fifth of everything. The victory at Badr is known to have had great importance for Muhammad. It assured him that Allah was with him.

From the beginning there was opposition from the Jews and the Jewish community toward Muhammad and his claim of being a prophet. They knew he could not be their Messiah since he was not an offspring of the family of David. Division between the two communities increased after some followers of Muhammad assassinated some Jews, and Muhammad and his followers made several attacks on the Jewish tribes. Among these tribes were Banu Qainuqa, Banu Nadir and Banu Quraizah, all of whom suffered great losses in these battles. In the battle against Banu Quraiza, the Muslim forces massacred some one thousand Jewish men. Their women and children were sold into slavery, and their property was divided among the Muslim soldiers.

In the year 628, the sixth year of *Hijra,* a treaty was made between the Quraish in Mecca and Muhammad and his followers. Both sides agreed to keep peace and not fight for a period of ten years. According to this treaty, Muhammad and his followers were allowed to visit Mecca and make pilgrimages in peace. Two years later Muhammad broke the treaty by attacking Mecca with an army of ten thousand men and taking control of the city. He destroyed all the images and idols in Ka'aba and executed some of the people.

By now Muhammad had become the undisputed political and religious leader of Arabia, and Mecca was the center of Islam. Upon receiving a modified revelation, from "let there be no compulsion in religion" (Sura 2:256) to "kill those who join other gods" (Sura 9:5), many tribes in Arabia could no longer resist Muhammad, but were forced to surrender, convert and submit to Islam and to Muhammad as its prophet. It was conversion to Islam or death.

Islam developed from a small sect into a major Arabian power. One generation later it had become a vast Arab empire, and in another two or three generations Islam had turned into a cosmopolitan civilization stretching across three continents, absorbing the heritage of many different cultures.

In the year 632, the tenth year of *Hijra,* Muhammad died. After his death, a power struggle ensued among his followers, leading to division and warfare among Muslims. Several different sects branched out within Islam. The Shia (or Shiites) and the Sunnites became the two major groups.

Expansion of Islam

By the time of Muhammad's death in 632, Islam had

become a dominant power in the Arabian peninsula. Muhammad's successors (caliphs) were appointed by the Muslim community to carry out the leadership and rule of Islam throughout the Arabian peninsula and other parts of the world.

The caliphs were more political figures than spiritual leaders. By military force the first caliph, Abu Bakr, brought all the tribes in the Arabian peninsula under the rule of Islam. These tribes had been divided after Muhammad's death.

Under the second caliph Omar (634–644) a phenomenal expansion began, which continued for about a hundred years. The Muslim armies defeated the armies of the Sassanian (Persian) and Byzantine empires. The Muslims then swept through the area that is present-day Iraq and Iran to Central Asia (Bukhara and Samarkand) and the Punjab. They conquered all the Asiatic territories of the Roman Empire except Anatolia (modern Turkey). Northward they occupied Syria, and Damascus was the capital of the Umayyad Dynasty (661-750). They conquered Egypt and moved across North Africa and into Europe, ruling most of Spain. Their move into the West was stopped in 732 by Charles Martel at the Battle of Tours in France. Thus, Islam was established in Africa, Middle East and Asia.

Within a hundred years after Muhammad's death, Islam became an empire in which Allah and the laws of Islam ruled from the Punjab to the Pyrenees, and from Samarkand to the Sahara.

Division Within Islam

After the assassination of Othman, the third caliph, in 656, increasing tension arose within the Muslim community. This ended in a civil war and division which still exists up to this present day throughout the Muslim world.

The Shiites, the followers of Ali, the fourth caliph, became strong opposers of the Umayyads (the tribe from which the third caliph came). The power struggle between these two Muslim groups continued after Ali's assassination in 661 by his former followers called Kharijites.

The killing, hatred and division went on as Yazid, the son of Mu'awiyah of the Umayyad Dynasty, massacred Hussein, the son of Ali, with his family in 680. This event is celebrated every year during the Islamic month of Moharram by Shiites. It is a time of mourning in commemoration of Imam Hussein and his family, and involves countless passion plays and penitential processions. The Shiites continued their revolt against the Umayyad Dynasty but with no success.

The Umayyad Dynasty lasted for nearly one hundred years (661–750). The successor dynasty, Abbasid caliphate (750–1258), brought the rule of Islam into a new dimension of political power and wealth. Baghdad, the capital of the Abbasid caliphs, became a major center for the political and economical activity of the empire. During this period the Islamic community experienced a renaissance in art, craft, education, science, commerce and law. It was a period of cultural glitter for the Islamic community.

By the end of the tenth century, the caliphs lost their political power, and the empire began to break up into smaller provinces led by governors and warlords. Different political and religious views caused more division within the Islamic community.

In 1258 Baghdad fell under the Mongol army. The Mongol invasion was devastating. However, the Muslims converted their Mongol and Tatar conquerors, and by the fifteenth century the Islamic community had recovered.

From the fifteenth to the eighteenth centuries Islam expanded to many new territories around the world. The political power of the Islamic community rose to new heights again with the uprising of three new empires — the Mughal in India, the Safavieh in Iran and the Ottoman in Anatolia (Turkey). These three empires had control over most of North Africa, the Middle East, Turkey, India and central Asia. During the reign of these three empires, Islam spread throughout many new regions in Africa, Asia and the Middle East, and many were converted to Islam.

The Ottoman Empire was the most aggressive of them all and was the leading force against the Byzantine Empire. By the end of the thirteenth century the Ottomans had conquered several Byzantine provinces, including Greece and Bulgaria. Constantinople, long a bulwark of Christendom against the Muslim advance, fell in 1453 and became Istanbul, the capital of the Ottoman Empire.

During the fifteenth and sixteenth centuries the Ottoman Turkish Empire continued to expand. Under Suleiman the Magnificent (1520–1566), it included all of the Balkan peninsula, except rugged Montenegro and a strip of the Dalmatian coast. It reached into Hungary, made the Black Sea a Turkish lake, and embraced Asia Minor, Armenia, Georgia, the Euphrates valley, Syria, Palestine, Egypt and the north coast of Africa as far as Morocco. The Ottoman Empire's advance to the West was stopped at the gates of Vienna in 1529, but it expanded southeastward, occupying Iraq and parts of Arabia.

Many areas where Christianity had been the faith of the majority now became predominantly Muslim. Christian communities survived but mainly in the historic Greek cities on the coast and among the Armenians. Systematic and compulsory conversion to Islam was common. Many Christian slaves of Muslim masters conformed to the faith of their owners.

In the Balkan peninsula, some of the Bogomils became Muslims to escape persecution by Orthodox and Catholic Christians. Thousands of sons of Christians were torn from their parents, reared as Muslims, and enrolled in the armies. Many churches were transformed into mosques.

The Safavieh and Mughal Empires fell in the eighteenth and nineteenth centuries respectively. The Ottoman Empire remained strong for a century and half. Their siege of Vienna in 1683 failed as it had in 1529. By 1699 the Ottomans had suffered several defeats by the Holy Alliance of Austria, Poland, Venice and the Russians. Greece became independent in 1829, and Algeria was occupied by the French in 1830. In 1922 the Ottoman Empire was abolished and was replaced by the Turkish republic.

The eighteenth and nineteenth centuries became an era of European colonization of the Muslim states. By the beginning of 1900 there were few Islamic states which were not dominated by the West. The British and French took control of most of the Islamic world. However, the days of colonialism were short-lived, and before World War II most of the former colonies gained formal independence. Nearly all the remainder became independent after the war and joined the United Nations — Iraq in 1932, Syria in 1947, Indonesia in 1950, Egypt in 1952, Morocco, Tunisia and Sudan in 1956, Malaysia in 1957, Nigeria in 1960 and Algeria in 1962.

Twentieth-Century Advance

The second half of the twentieth century brought a new identity and strength to the Islamic world. Oil became the booster of the economic growth of many of these newly independent Islamic states. The oil embargo of 1973 caused tremendous concern in the West; it brought the realization of the great strength and political power of the Islamic states.

The majority of these states were supported by Western governments. Oil was traded for military equipment and Western technology. The Western influence upon these secular, pro-Western governments paved the way for the resurgence of conservative Islamic values. To the conservatives, the Western lifestyle was a threat to the Islamic community and its law.

In many of these states, increasing inflation, unemployment, governmental corruption, and the lack of political freedom and human rights set the stage for the revival of Islam.

Some leaders of these Islamic states, such as the Shah of Iran and Anwar Sadat in Egypt, had not paid much attention to the increasing disillusionment of their citizens. For the younger, educated generation, two options were available to obtain freedom from the oppression of their governments — communism or fundamentalist Islam. Although communism found its way in through the back doors of universities and colleges throughout these states, Islam had greater success. Islam had deeper roots in their societies and a fiercer history of warfare against tyranny than communism did.

Thus, the beginning of the second half of the twentieth century brought a new wind of Islamic fundamentalism, with many fundamentalist groups sprouting up throughout the Middle East and North Africa. In 1993 *Time* magazine reported, "A tide of religious fervor has been sweeping across the Islamic belt, threatening to turn half a dozen countries into theocratic states akin to Iran, Sudan and Afghanistan. Terrorism, intolerance and revolution for export are some of the by-products."[1]

The Islamic revolution of 1979 in Iran led by Khomeini further revived the radical and militant Islamic movement. There were also other factors which contributed to the resurgence of Islamic fundamentalism in the twentieth century, including the situation of the Palestinians, the occupation of the Islamic country of Afghanistan by Soviet communists and the rise of Saddam Hussein in Iraq.

During the past few decades Islam has escalated almost to its original state of ideology within the Muslim community, and outwardly Islam is reaching to a tremendous height of expansion in the world.

During the past forty years, millions of Muslims have been emigrating to the West. In America, England, France, Holland and many other Western European countries the number of Muslims exceeds that of many religious minority groups. In some areas there are more Muslims than Christian denominational groups. George Otis, in his book *The Last of the Giants*, points out the following information. In the United States, for instance, Muslims currently outnumber members of the Assemblies of God three to one.[2] The United Kingdom now has more followers of Allah than Methodists and Baptists combined.[3] In France, Muslims are the nation's second-largest religious group and have more adherents than all Protestant denominations put together.[4]

With the tide of millions of Muslim immigrants, Islam received another chance at expansion throughout Europe, a continent where Islam previously had little success. Muslims now believe that if they can win London to Islam, it will not be hard to win Western Europe.

It seems that they do not take this matter lightly. In 1945 there was only one mosque in England. The number grew to twenty-five in 1950, to eighty by 1960 and to two hundred mosques by 1976. By the year 1989 the number of mosques in England was more than one thousand.[5] Three hundred of the buildings used for mosques were originally churches. Even the church that sent William Carey to India was converted to a mosque.[6]

According to an ABC report by Peter Jennings, more than five thousand mosques were built in the southern republics of the CIS (the former Soviet Union) within two years after their independence.

In East and West Africa so many mosques are being built

that it is difficult to know the exact number. In Kenya alone the Muslims' goal is to build one mosque every ten kilometers whether there are Muslims in the area or not.[7]

Countries like Iran, Saudi Arabia, Libya and Turkey are pouring millions of dollars into the southern republics of former Soviet Union and into African countries with the intent of expanding Islam.

Whether by the force of the sword or the wealth of oil, Muslims are winning fifty million people annually to their faith. After Christianity, Islam is the fastest growing religion on the face of the earth.[8]

THREE

ISLAM AND VIOLENCE

LET AMERICA, ISRAEL AND THE world know that we have a lust for martyrdom and our motto is being translated into reality."

These were the words of Sheikh Mohammed Yazbeck in a rally in Baalbeck a week after the bombing of the U.S. Marines battalion headquarters in Lebanon.[1]

A Bloodthirsty Spirit

Islam has left a fingerprint of blood through every page of its history, beginning with *Hijra* up to this very day.

The spirit that advocated Islam is a bloodthirsty spirit which rages war and division. It is a spirit of revenge and retaliation. Its purpose is to create hate, sorrows, mourning and confusion. The following statement by Hussein Musawi, the leader of the Islamic Amal movement, illustrates such a spirit:

> This path is the path of blood, the path of martyrdom. For us death is easier than smoking a cigarette if it comes while fighting for the cause of God and while defending the oppressed.[2]

Where this spirit is permitted, there will be terror and fear. This spirit feeds on fear and death — the very work and nature of Satan.

Though Muslim scholars try to justify the acts, teachings and laws of Islam, they cannot deny the history of bloodshed that Islam has left upon the pages of human history.

Khomeini's Example

One of the most vigorous acts of this bloodthirsty spirit has taken place in the country of Iran where the undeniable brutality and grim reign of the Islamic fundamentalists illustrate the hideous nature of Islam. The brutality is to such an extent that even some of the former top officials of this regime have acknowledged it.

Bani-Sadr, the first president of the Islamic Republic of Iran and a former strong admirer of Khomeini, was ousted and had to flee to exile in Paris, where he called on Iranians to "rise and resist. Overthrow this regime which has proven more bloodthirsty than the monarchy."[3]

Soon after the return of Khomeini to Iran and the establishment of an Islamic republic, a separation and division began among the people in Iran. Many political parties and groups were established — Marxists and Leninists, Maoists, right-wingers and left-wingers. Many branches sprang up from within Islam: the moderates, revolutionaries, extremists and fanatics. These groups continuously fought and clashed.

Finally, Khomeini and his government took control and came down hard on everything that was not according to the Islamic Shari'a (Islamic law and tradition). This crackdown rated to the extent of terrors, executions, bomb explosions, murder and other atrocities.

Mojahedin, an Islamic fundamentalist organization with a leftist ideology, was one of the organizations Khomeini targeted. Mojahedin consisted predominantly of young, revolutionary ideologists who were also involved in a very active guerrilla movement against the former Shah of Iran's government.

The ruthless crackdown against the Mojahedin started in 1981 by the military and the revolutionary police. Prisons overflowed with men and women ranging in age from twelve to seventy-five. On June 20, 1981, the Islamic government of Ayatollah began a reign of terror and executions of the Mojahedin. By December of that year the government had executed some twenty-five hundred Mojahedin followers. Some were hanged; others were put before the firing squads. Sometimes the bodies of these people were left on public gallows.[4]

Robin Wright, an American educator and correspondent journalist for several national and international papers, records the following in her book, *In the Name of God:*

> Many times the only way families knew what had happened to their loved ones was by reading newspaper columns listing the latest executions, although not all the names were revealed. The subsequent crackdown was so brutal that it quickly became known as the reign of terror, a term adapted from similar eras under Robespierre in France and Stalin in the Soviet Union.[5]

A well-known Muslim saying states, "One must wash blood with blood." Hatred and bloodshed continued as the Mojahedin countered state terror with its own brand of terror. They carried out daily assassination attacks on the high-ranking officials of the government in every major city of the country. Hundreds were blown to pieces by these merciless suicide attacks. The majority of these suicide assassins were young, aged fifteen to twenty-five.

On September 11, 1981, a twenty-two-year-old Mojahed man attended the Friday prayer at Tabriz. He walked up to Ayatollah Baha al-Din Madani and exploded two hand grenades, killing himself, his intended victim and seventeen *pasdars* (special policemen who enforce Islamic law). Two weeks after this incident, a seventeen-year-old high school student blew up himself and Hojjat al-Islam Hasheminezhad, the Islamic Republic Party leader in the city of Khorasan.[6]

The bloodshed between the Islamic government of Khomeini and the Mojahedin continued for four years, taking the lives of 12,250 political dissidents, three-quarters of whom were Mojahedin members or sympathizers.[7]

Exposing the Ideology

The way some of these people were killed is so hideous that mention of it brings total horror to one's mind. The only explanation for the inhuman acts of these people is the ideology which has brought them to such a level of hate, fear and death.

Both Khomeini's people and the Mojahedins identify themselves as strong, devout followers of Shia. (Shia is a branch of Islam. Followers of Shia are also referred to as Shiites. Their heroes are Muhammad, the prophet of Islam, and Hussein, his grandson, who is known as the Sayyid ash-Shuhada ("Lord of Martyrs"). The assassinations, killing, murdering and suicide missions are justified by pointing back to A.D. 680 murder of Hussein with some seventy-two of his followers, including women and children, in the plain of Karbala by the Umayyad caliph Yazid. To these Muslim groups, Hussein was the ultimate martyr who fought despite the foreknowledge that he and his family would face a bloody defeat.

To the Shiite, Hussein is an example of justice and the uncompromising battle against the unjust reign of the wicked rulers. Shiites want justice, and they are willing to shed blood for it. They believe that there is no other way of establishing justice except through bloodshed.

Iranian-born Ervand Abrahamian in his book, *The Iranian Mojahedin,* describes the Mojahedin declaration of the June 20, 1981, massacre by the Islamic government:

> Khordad 30th (20 June 1981) is our Ashura. On that day we had to stand up and resist Khomeini's bloodthirsty and reactionary regime, even if it meant sacrificing our lives and the whole of our organization. We had to take this road to Karbala to keep alive our tawhidi ideology, follow the example set by Imam Hussein, fulfill our historic mission to the Iranian people, and fight the most bloodthirsty, most reactionary, and most savage regime in world history.[8]

The same spirit and almost the same words are uttered through the lips of Iran's Ayatollah Khomeini, who was marked by the Mojahedin as an enemy of the true Islam:

> But our nation is no longer ready to submit to humiliation and abjection; it prefers a bloody death to a life of shame. We are ready to be killed, and we have made a covenant with God to follow the path of our leader, the Lord of Martyrs.[9]

Dying to Please Allah

To a Muslim, dying and killing for the cause of Islam is not only an honor, but also a way of pleasing Allah. The only way Muslims can have assurance of salvation and eternal life is by becoming a martyr for the cause of Islam. This is why so many young boys in Iran volunteered to become a *basiji* ("the mobilized").

Khomeini went on television asking for ten thousand volunteers to fight in the war. The next day all the boys on the street who had volunteered had a piece of red tape on their foreheads. Their task would be to die for the cause.

A *basiji* was committed to death, not just the possibility of death. The *basijis* volunteered to clear the minefields with their bodies, and they did it. Military leaders would send out as many as five thousand boys at once to run through the fields and trip the mines. Sometimes they asked the boys to clear high voltage border fences by throwing their bodies against the fences,

Thousands of young bodies were shattered and electrocuted in this manner. Many of the boys were only twelve or thirteen years old. To them, Khomeini gave the promise of *behesht* ("paradise"). To symbolize this false promise, he gave them a key which they hung around their neck — a key with which they could open the gate of heaven.

A note left by one young Iranian soldier, Mohsen Naeemi, who died in the war with Iraq, reflects the mind of Islam and the deception of this religion.

> My wedding is at the front and my bride is martyrdom. The sermon will be uttered by the roar of guns. I shall attire myself in my blood for this ceremony. My bride, martyrdom, shall give birth to my son, freedom. I leave this son in your safekeeping. Keep him well.[10]

41

I know of a fourteen-year-old boy who volunteered to be a *basiji* for his country. For four years, his family believed he was dead, but his body was never found. They assumed his body had been blown apart when he triggered a land mine, which was what had happened to so many others.

But four years later the boy came home. He was not dead. He had made it through the minefield and was captured by enemy troops and put in jail. They fed him water, potato skins and eggplant skins for four years. So from age fourteen to age eighteen, he lived in a prison and suffered.

One Western official remarked:

> As we are learning, these are not the odd men out. Whatever hardship stories come out of Iran, it remains a source of pride to the Shia....They truly live in a different world, their thinking totally alien and incomprehensible to the Western mind. We keep thinking they will come to their senses and realize this foolhardiness will cost them their one and only life. What is hard for us to fathom is that this is what life is all about to them, a gateway to heaven that must be earned.[11]

For Khomeini, the death of these young people of Iran was not a loss, but an asset. Khomeini's message to Saddam Hussein was, "We should sacrifice all our loved ones for the sake of Islam. If we are killed, we have performed our duty."[12]

Khomeini truly fulfilled this proclamation during the eight-year war with Iraq. I was told by many Iranians that finding a husband in Iran after the war was a miracle because there weren't many young men left alive.

True Islam Is Militant

Some may argue that Khomeini, with his militant Shiite

beliefs, did not represent true Islam, that a true Muslim is not militant. On the contrary, this is the very nature and teaching of Islam. Islam's history reveals that Khomeini's twentieth-century expression of Islam was born in seventh-century Arabia and later enforced upon other people in other countries around the world.

In his book *The Hokumat-e-Islami (Islamic Rule),* Khomeini clearly identifies his ideologies, claims and views as a revival of a tradition he traces to Muhammad, the prophet of Islam. A scholar commented regarding Khomeini, "[He] defines Islamic identity in terms of paradigm or an archetype provided by the activity of the Prophet Muhammad, Imam Ali and Imam Hussein."[13]

Many Muslims around the world who have realized the grim and merciless acts of the Islamic Republic of Iran have tried to separate Islam from Khomeini's version of it. Many scholars and writers have made the same vain attempt. They try to justify Islam by labeling the Islamic revolution of Iran as an extremist version of Islam. Their assessment is no more than a lack of knowledge of history and a lack of understanding of the nature of Islam.

The violence and bloodshed is not exclusive to the Islam of the Shiites as some try to claim. Many Muslim fundamentalists throughout the Middle East and North Africa are not Shiites, yet their deeds and actions are identical to those witnessed in the Islamic revolution in Iran.

The Muslim Brotherhood in Egypt and Syria is one example. This organization was founded by Hassan al Banna (1904–1949) in 1928 in Egypt with the goal of returning to the fundamentals of true Islam. The movement expanded in membership as persecution from the Egyptian government increased. The Brotherhood became more and more militant; they trained their young members for *jihad* ("holy war") against British colonialists. They also prepared to help the Palestinians against the Israelis. Their slogan was,

"The Koran is our constitution, the Prophet is our guide; Death for the glory of Allah is our greatest ambition."[14]

The following, recorded by Robin Wright in her book *Sacred Rage,* explains the spirit of hate and bloodshed in the Muslim Brotherhood:

> A former Egyptian Interior Minister, Ahmed Mortada al Maraghi, wrote about how the young militants were recruited:
> A small room lit with candle light and smoky with incense is chosen...Once the likely young man is selected, he is brought to this room...where he will find a sheikh repeating verses from the Koran...The Sheikh with eyes like magnets stares at the young man who is paralyzed with awe...They will then pray, and the sheikh will recite verses from the Koran about those fighting for the sake of Allah and are therefore promised to go to heaven. "Are you ready for martyrdom?" the young man is asked. "Yes, yes," he repeats. He is then given the oath on the Koran. These young men leave the meeting with one determination: to kill.[15]

Out of the Muslim Brotherhood organization, many other radical groups sprouted in Egypt. Groups like Al Jihad ("The Jihad Organization") and Al Taqfir Wal Higrah ("Repentance and Migration") are responsible for the assassination of many innocent people. Their nature is truly demonstrated in how they kill their victims. Sheikh Mohammad al Dhahabi, the minister of religious endowment of Egypt, was among the victims assassinated by Al Taqfir Wal Higrah. He was first strangled, then a bullet was fired into his left eye.[16]

Al Jihad is known as the organization responsible for the 1981 assassination of Egyptian President Anwar Sadat and seven others. Sheik Omar Abdel Rahman, one of the recognized spiritual leaders of Al Jihad, was arrested, imprisoned, then acquitted, for encouraging the assassination.

Time magazine says of Abdel Rahman:

> U.S. and Egyptian officials suspect him of issuing *fatwas,* or religious decrees, in the 1990 Manhattan slaying of Jewish militant Rabbi Meir Kahane and the 1992 Brooklyn murder of an Egyptian named Mustafa Shalabi...Cairo officials also blame Sheik Omar and his 10,000 hard-core disciples in Egypt for 20 attacks against tourist targets....Islamic groups, of which Sheik Omar's is just one of many, have accelerated their attacks on security forces and Coptic Christians, as well as tourist sites. Last year 80 people were killed and 130 wounded.[17]

In the same article Sheik Omar explained his view:

> I just want to serve Islam by all my strength and power. Khomeini led a revolution and beautified his country, made it clean of Shah, who was so unjust. What Khomeini did was a real success.[18]

Islamic organizations like Mojahedin, Hamaz, Hezbollah, Amal, the Palestinian Liberation Organization (PLO) and others have proven that war and bloodshed are distinct patterns for a true Islam.

Mohammed Taki Moudarrissi, another leader of the Islamic Amal movement, has stated, "I can in one week assemble five hundred faithful ready to throw themselves into suicide operations. No frontier will stop them."[19]

The Spirit of Fear

Fear is the stronghold of any false religion and the very

foundation of any demonic cult. If a false religion stands strong, it is because that religion exercises great fear over its adherents. In other words, fear is the life sap of a false religion.

Fear is a darkroom in which Satan develops his negatives. Fear is the strongest weapon Satan has used against mankind. Fear of death is the strongest form of bondage. The purpose of fear is manipulation and control. The person caught in the snare of fear is controlled by the forces of darkness.

Communism is an excellent example. This ideology, actually a form of religion, intensely controlled multitudes of people by the power of fear. For seventy years nations and people of different nationalities were controlled by the fear of this force.

Communism was not a physical force, but a spiritual force. The very people in charge and in authority over this system were in a bondage of fear themselves. People living under a communistic government feared one another on a constant basis.

When I first traveled to the country of Romania in 1989, it was still under the Ceausescu regime. I felt the presence of fear everywhere I went. It was so strong that you could reach out and touch it. Everyone feared everyone else. The air was filled with the heaviness of that spirit. To be honest, I felt it when the plane crossed over the Austrian sky into the Romanian sky. I could tell that something was different even though we had not yet landed.

The border police made us shiver by just looking our way. They were representatives of their government. That spirit which was over their leaders was also over them.

By traveling through these Eastern European countries, we often noticed the expressions on people's faces. They were in fear and in sadness, held captive by the forces of darkness. Oh, praise be to God who destroyed the power and stronghold of communism! Once that spirit was bound and cast out, it could no longer hold people in slavery. The strongman of communism was defeated, and the chains of fear were broken. Once people realized that communism was dead, they feared it no more.

Observing the fruits of Islam and the Muslim communities, one will realize that Islam is another force that holds people in the stronghold of fear. From its beginning to this day, fear of death has been the strategy of Islam in expanding and making converts. Sura 9:5 of the Koran, the holy book of Islam, says:

> When the sacred months are past, kill those who join other gods wherever you find them, and seize them, beleaguer them, and lie in wait for them with every kind of ambush; but if they convert and observe prayer and pay the obligatory alms, let them go their way.

Pagans were forced at the point of the sword to become Muslims. The choice was either to become a Muslim or die:

> O Prophet, strive hard against the unbelievers and the hypocrites, and be firm against them. Their abode is Hell, an evil refuge indeed (Sura 9:73).

From the time of *Hijra,* when Muhammad and his followers emigrated from Mecca to Medina in A.D. 622, up to this hour, terror and fear have been the strategy of Islam. Daily news reports of the terrorist activities of the Hezbollah ("party of God") in Lebanon; the Hamaz, the Islamic terror organization in Israel; and the Muslim Brotherhood in Egypt are proof of this fact. Men like Khomeini, Saddam, Ghadafi, Idi Amin and many other Islamic leaders are feared by millions of people.

Within two years of the establishment of the Islamic government of the Ayatollah Khomeini, such an atmosphere of terror and fear was created by the Islamic clerics that the first prime minister of the Islamic Republic of Iran, Mehdi Bazargan, who resigned after nine months, described the situation of the country in an open letter. In it Bazargan charged the government with creating "an atmosphere of terror, fear, revenge and national disintegration." He continued:

> What has the ruling elite done besides bring death and destruction, pack the prisons and cemeteries in every city, create long queues, shortage, high prices, unemployment, poverty, homeless people, repetitious slogans and a dark future?[20]

Bazargan's description of the reign of the Islamic government is a valid description of many Islamic governments throughout the world who are true to Islamic values. The countries that will follow the laws of Islam (as they are) will have the same result as Iran has had under the leadership of Khomeini. That is because Khomeini's ideology is the true Islam.

I worked for four years (1983–1987) among the Iranian refugees throughout Europe. During that time I came across many hurting and confused people. Thousands upon thousands of well-educated people, young and old, had to leave Iran because their lives were threatened by the regime of Khomeini. Many of them had come very close to death, either in the jails of the Islamic republic or in their flight from the country. Their stories were unbelievable; the majority of them could write a thrilling best-seller with fear of death as the theme. As one Iranian man told me one day, "It is as though death and fear rules over that nation."

The Bible says that through fear of death people are subject to bondage all their lifetime (Heb. 2:15). By creating terror and death, Islam has been able to control and bind some one billion people around the world. This has been the very strategy of Islam throughout history. The story of Salman Rushdie, the British author who lived in hiding because he feared that his life would be taken by Muslims, portrays the hideous nature of the fear created by Islam.

Thus Islam holds its followers in the bondage and shackles of fear. They fear Allah, and they fear the devil and the demons (*jinn*). Islam plunges Muslims into a state of fear where denial of Islam means death and the wrath of Allah.

FOUR

ISLAM IN AMERICA

ACCORDING TO A RECENT GALLUP poll, the number of American Muslims is growing rapidly. The *Yearbook of American and Canadian Churches 1993* indicates that there are six million Muslims in America.[1] According to *Scholastic Update*, Islam has now become the fastest growing religion in the United States. Of the eleven hundred mosques in America, 80 percent have been built within the last twelve years.[2] Many sources indicate that in just a few years, Muslims in the United States will outnumber Jews, if this is not already the case.

Why Islam Is Growing?

The dramatic increase of the Muslim population in the

United States in the past few decades is due to several factors.

1. A flood of Muslim immigrants to the United States

The ratification of the 1965 Immigration Act by President Lyndon Johnson caused an increase in the number of non-European immigrants, many from the Muslim nations. Since 1965, waves of Muslim immigrants have flooded the shores of this nation. Big cities like New York, Los Angeles, Chicago, Houston, Dallas and Washington have become home to many Muslim immigrants from Africa, the Middle East and East Asia. They came for a better life and a better future.

Several hundred thousand Afghan refugees who had fought the Communists fled persecutions and war and came to America. They were considered by President Reagan as friends of America. Over two million Iranians, the majority of whom were highly educated and financially well off, fled Iran and the wrath of a grim regime and came to America.[3] Others, like the Lebanese and people from the former Yugoslavia, came to America because of civil war in their homelands.

They came, bringing their religion and faith with them. New York, for instance, is a mecca of Muslim believers. Entire neighborhoods in Brooklyn and the Bronx are populated by Muslims. According to the Islamic Mission of America, there are 2.5 million Muslims in the New York metropolitan region.[4]

Many new centers, mosques and Islamic schools are popping up all over the United States. These Islamic centers or places which serve as mosques began appearing in the 1920s and 1930s. In 1952 there were just more than twenty mosques in the United States. By 1992 the number of mosques and Islamic centers had grown to more than twenty-three hundred.[5]

Financial aid from Islamic foreign embassies is the backbone of many of these new mosques, schools and Islamic centers. Saudi Arabia alone has spent $87 billion since 1973 to spread Islam throughout the United States and the Western hemisphere.[6] Other countries including Iraq, Libya, Kuwait and Iran have poured millions and millions of dollars into the West for the same purpose. The president of a large Islamic school in Los Angeles claims that government officials from Saudi Arabia, Iraq and Kuwait have offered to subsidize his organization. A group of Iranian businessmen offered him $1 million if he would admit to them that he was a Shiite.[7]

King Fahd of Saudi Arabia has committed $7 to $8 million to build a new mosque at the site of Masjid Bilal, the African American mosque in Los Angeles.[8] From 1979 to 1981, the Saudis gave $10 million to spread Islam in the United States, and they have reportedly given millions more since.[9]

2. High birthrates within Muslim families

Those from the Middle East enjoy large families as a cultural tradition. They do not think as much about the expenses of having children as people do in the West. The teachings of Islam are carefully passed on to the next generation.

3. The conversion of many African Americans to Islam

Not only have the numbers of Muslim immigrants to the United States been on the rise in recent years, many Americans are also converting to Islam. Sixty to 90 percent of all converts to Islam in the United States are African American. Eighty percent of these converts were raised in the church.[10] The exact number of African American converts is not known; estimates range from five hundred thousand to 1.5 million.[11]

Carl Ellis, the founder of Project Joseph, a ministry that educates Christians about Islam, reports that there were four hundred thousand African American converts to Islam in 1991. By 1995 there were 1.2 million African Americans converts to Islam.[12] This is a 300 percent increase in four years. *Christianity Today* reported, "If the conversion rate continues unchanged, Islam could become the dominant religion in Black urban areas by the year 2020."[13]

The majority of the African American converts are Sunni Muslims. There are, of course, several different groups and sects within the African American Islamic community. Nation of Islam is the most visible sect, mainly because of the attention given by the media to its leader, Louis Farrakhan.

The Black Muslim Movement

The spread of Islam among African Americans began in 1913. Timothy Drew Ali, who founded the Moorish Science Temple in New Jersey, is believed to be the first American convert to Islam. He introduced Islam to many blacks. Out of that movement other groups like the Nation of Islam (NOI) were brought forth. NOI has its origin in a sect founded in Detroit in 1930 by W. D. Fard, also known as Fard Muhammad. Fard taught that black people were the original people, the first rulers of earth. They were stolen by the white man and brought to a life of slavery in North America. Fard believed that the black people had to be reconverted to their original religion, Islam, speak their original language, Arabic, and change their names to Islamic names.

Fard believed that the white man is not truly human or a direct creation of God, but a race of devils. The white man and all other non-black races were products of an experiment in prehistoric times on the Island of Patmos by a black scientist named Mr. Yakub. The white race was then given six thousand years to rule the earth, and the Original People (the black race) were put to sleep.

Allah then came to his nation (people) in the person of Fard Muhammad to resurrect them. Eventually Allah will destroy the devils (white people) from the earth and transform the universe into a black paradise where justice and equality will prevail.

Among the people who followed Fard's teachings was Elijah Poole, the son of a black Baptist preacher from Georgia. He later changed his name to Elijah Muhammad and became the well-known leader of the NOI. In 1934, Fard disappeared mysteriously, and Elijah took over the NOI. Under his leadership the organization expanded. Elijah taught that Allah appeared in the person of Fard, and that he himself was a prophet of Allah.

Elijah Muhammad constructed a new religion of strict discipline and a self-sufficient community with black power and rights. They established schools known as Universities of Islam. They also formed their own army known as the Fruit of Islam (FOI). NOI was soon recognized as a dangerous, racist and hateful organization that concerned Washington. NOI and its leaders were under active surveillance by the FBI.

In 1975 Elijah Muhammad died of heart failure and was succeeded by his son, Warith Deen Muhammad, also known as Imam Muhammad. He made radical changes in the organization, merging more of the faith of orthodox Sunni Islam into NOI. He also dissolved the army. During this transformation process NOI lost many members. The organization, however, regained its strength under its new leader, Louis Farrakhan.

Louis Farrakhan

Farrakhan came into the national limelight as a supporter of Rev. Jesse Jackson during Jackson's bid for presidential nominee of the Democratic Party in 1984 and 1988. Farrakhan's Syrian connections helped Jackson free the captured American Navy pilot Lt. Robert Goodman, Jr. on January 3, 1984.

Louis Wilcott Farrakhan was born in 1933 in Bronx, New York. Farrakhan, a talented musician, came in contact with Elijah Muhammad in 1955 in Chicago. He soon abandoned his musical carrier and joined NOI. Farrakhan served as a lieutenant and later captain of the FOI and also as the minister of the Boston Mosque.

After Elijah's death there was an ideological division within NOI. Farrakhan's stand was more towards Elijah Muhammad's Islam than the orthodox Islamic faith espoused by Elijah's son, Imam Muhammad. In an interview Farrakhan said, "Elijah Muhammad never intended for us to follow completely what is called orthodox Islam."[14] In a speech on November 8, 1977, Farrakhan officially declared his intention to reestablish the Nation of Islam "on the platform of the Elijah Muhammad."[15]

Farrakhan's charisma and leadership brought new acceptance of the Nation of Islam within the black community. The Nation of Islam has gained many new converts in recent years with its appeal of black pride and black empowerment.

An Open Door for Islam

Segregation, social injustice, police brutality, poverty and decaying ghetto life were the elements that opened the door for Islam's infiltration into the black urban areas. Social injustice spiced with racial oppression is always fertile ground for the advancement of a religion like Islam among the oppressed.

Malcolm X, who was assassinated in 1964, was one of the strongest voices of the Black Muslim movement. To men like him and Farrakhan, Islam was and is a way through which the black man could experience freedom from a brutal, unjust system. Islam gave them hope of protection and pride, a voice for their anger and frustration at injustice.

Islam's God displays a militant wrath against the oppressor; it takes the side of the weak and the oppressed, and fights with hate and anger against the oppressor. Islam demands justice and vengeance, an eye for an eye and a tooth for a tooth. It is a religion of rebellion of the oppressed against the oppressor.

Islam stands at the opposite pole of Christianity. To Muslims, Christianity is a naive and weak sort of belief. A man who turns the other cheek in the face of the oppressor is deceived and powerless. Islam gives the right to defend oneself from the oppressor: "And those [believers] who, when an oppressive wrong is inflicted on them, (are not cowed but) help and defend themselves" (Sura 42:39).

Freedom and Justice

Within the human spirit there is a longing for liberty and freedom. Man was made in the likeness of God, in the righteousness of God, which is all the rightness of God. It is contrary to man's makeup and nature to be oppressed because of the color of his skin, his culture or his background because that's who he is, and he is made in God's image. Man was not made to be dominated, but to dominate. Slavery and segregation were the result of a demon assault against the creation of God.

The black man, who was made into the image of God, had become enslaved by hatred and oppressed by an unjust system. A man in this condition, such as the black man was during slavery and segregation, will either revolt and demand his liberty, or he will die with dignity. It would be unnatural for a man to do otherwise. "Give me liberty or give me death," as Patrick Henry said.

Man's spirit craves for freedom and justice. Man alone without an ideology or a deity as his supporter would be unable to pursue fully his freedom. Freedom without justice is a meaningless concept. Any movement which has captured the allegiance of the black man has espoused a burning desire for justice and liberty.

The Black Muslim movement in America started during the dark period of segregation. Blacks desired freedom from the oppressor and the restoration of their dignity.

The church in general failed to preach the values of black men who were made in the image of God. It failed to proclaim their freedom from segregation. The church failed to reach them and touch them and make them realize that they were loved by God and by His church.

The people in America who did speak out against segregation and injustice came mainly from within the African American communities. In a speech at the National Press Club in Washington, Martin Luther King, Jr. said, "The church is the most segregated major institute in America."[16]

This vacuum, created by the lack of knowledge of the love of God, opened the doors for deception and ungodly ideologies to become the higher authority for these freedom seekers. Thus, we saw the birth of many Black Muslim movements. Most of the militant black supremacist groups within the Islamic faith were raised up during the time of segregation: Nation of Islam (NOI), Five Percenters, Ansaar Allah, Islamic Party of North America, Dar ul-Islam, Islamic Brotherhood and the Hanafi Movement.

Even though segregation is officially abolished and the rights of African Americans are protected by the law, more African Americans now turn to the faith of Islam than they did during the time of Elijah Muhammad and Malcolm X. Many athletes, like Muhammad Ali, Mike Tyson and Kareem Abdul-Jabar, have turned to the Islamic faith.

I believe it is time for the church to ask why. Why is it

that Farrakhan with his most anti-Christian ideology can be invited to so many black churches throughout America? Farrakhan himself has said he has preached in as many churches as he has in mosques.[17] In the past few years, about two thousand Christian leaders have visited Farrakhan at his home in Chicago.[18] Why?

The Attraction of Islam

African Americans and Westerners are not attracted primarily to Islam's laws or history. Rather, their attraction to Islam is a revolt against powerless churches. Jesus said, "You are the salt of the earth; but if the salt loses its flavor, how shall it be seasoned? It is then good for nothing but to be thrown out and trampled underfoot by men" (Matt. 5:13).

Bridgett X Muldrow, a recent convert, says, "I had belonged to a Baptist church, but the mosque offered more for me. There was more togetherness and bonding in the mosque."[19] We are in bad shape when the mosque offers more love to the people than we as the followers of Christ do.

In America, many churches are still struggling with the issue of prejudice. The church remains fragmented in this area. Many churches have pulled their forces out to white suburbia rather than deal with the issues confronting America's urban ghettos. The church remains segregated — white congregations have few African American members, and black congregations have few white people in their congregations. No wonder Farrakhan preaches that Christianity is a white man's religion. Where did he get that? From the Bible? Or from the lifestyle of us Christians?

While the Nation of Islam and other Islamic groups invade the ghettos with a message of brotherhood and a helping hand to rid the neighborhoods of drugs, prostitution and a social welfare mentality, we are singing, "This little light of mine, I'm gonna let it shine," in fancy suburban churches.

Farrakhan addresses the needs of the black man in America. Many young African Americans are searching for their identity in a society flooded with racism and rejection. Many of these young kids have grown up in neighborhoods infested with drugs, crime, gang violence and poverty. They have no role model or father figure to follow. They are involved with gangs and crimes because they are craving acceptance and worth. Farrakhan and the Nation of Islam are giving that to them. This is why the NOI and other Islamic groups are especially successful in American prisons.

Men like Malcolm X still have an effect on the African American. Carl Ellis says, "Malcolm X's words continue to have a great impact on all blacks, not just Muslim blacks. He helped give a new meaning to being black."[20] Malcolm X's message to the black people was, "We all have in common the greatest binding tie we could have — we all are black people."[21]

Faheemah Sharrieff, an African American who was a convert to Islam for twenty-five years, says, "It was a thing that made us feel good about ourselves; it was a black identity thing. It gave us something we did not have — it gave us boldness and strength." Sharrieff, now a born-again Christian, points out that "not everything I learned in the Nation was bad. There was a respect for women among them, there was more sisterhood and brotherhood and discipline in the Nation."

Sharrieff was sixteen years old when she became a Muslim. "The Nation of Islam is attracting a lot of young people," Sharrieff claims. "While we go to church on Sundays, the Nation goes out to the streets to win the prostitutes, drug dealers and bums."[22] (Sharrieff's testimony is told in more detail in the last chapter of this book.)

Because of what has been done to the blacks in the past, it will take much more than what we as a church have done to gain back the trust of African Americans. People who share the feelings of Farrakhan and Malcolm X need to be treated with respect and equality.

The only place where people feel safe is where they are loved. The church is the only institution that can bring true healing, restoration, respect and worth to all races. People need to be touched and loved in the same way that Jesus touched us.

During a large meeting conducted by a white charismatic evangelist where I was personally present, the evangelist asked all the white folks turn to the black folks and ask them for forgiveness. Hugs were exchanged, and words of encouragement were spoken. I personally thought the whole thing seemed like superficial, emotional, mushy, charismatic fluff. Not that asking forgiveness was wrong, for there is a great need for that. But it takes more than hugs and kisses to heal a broken history. If we are to do away with racism and the advancements of black separatists and Islamic groups, it will take much more than hugs and kisses.

We shake hands and hug and say nice words, but our hearts can be miles apart. If our love is not real, they will recognize it. It is time for us to make an effort and touch our cities with the love of Jesus. The church needs to proclaim Jesus and demonstrate His power. If we do not, the vacuum will be filled by men like Elijah Muhammad, Malcolm X and Louis Farrakhan.

FIVE

ISLAM VERSUS
THE TRUTH OF CHRIST

SATAN IS A PERSONAL ENEMY of God, His people and His plan. The devil is an accuser, a slanderer, an adversary, a deceiver and an opposer. This is his nature. Whatever opposes the Word of God and assaults the Lord Jesus, originates, in my opinion, in one way or another from Satan.

Throughout history, we have seen that the people who have resisted God and His Word are mostly people with a religious covering. Jesus' greatest opponents in His time were the religious Jews. They were the ones who time after time opposed the words of Jesus and plotted against His life, finally handing Him over to the Romans to be hanged on the cross. Religion and religious people have always been the opposers of the truth. It seems as though religion is Satan's best partner in resisting the truth of God and His Son Jesus.

Writing to the churches in Galatia, the apostle Paul strictly warns:

> Even if we, or an angel from heaven, preach any other gospel to you than what we have preached to you, let him be accursed (Gal. 1:8).

The Galatians had mixed the gospel with the law in order to gain righteousness. Paul, inspired by the Holy Spirit, writes this forceful epistle to do away with the false gospel of works and demonstrate the superiority of justification by faith in Christ Jesus.

God curses any gospel other than the gospel of Jesus. I do not care how close it matches and how alike it may seem; it is not accepted. The difference between religion and Jesus is this: Religion is partially true, but Jesus is the whole truth. Anything less than Jesus is religion. I do not care if it's labeled Christianity or Islam or Hinduism or whatever.

Islam is a religion whose teachings contradict the very foundation of the gospel. Sura 61:9 and Sura 48:27-28 state that Islam is exalted above and over all religions, including Christianity.

Islam Denies the Death of Jesus

Islam denies the death and the resurrection of Jesus. It says in Sura 4:157, "That they said (in boast) 'We killed Christ Jesus, the son of Mary, the messenger of Allah,' but they killed him not, nor crucified him, but so it was made to appear to them."

When Jesus foretold His death and resurrection to His disciples in Matthew 16, Peter resisted Jesus' prophecy:

Then Peter took Him [Jesus] aside and began to rebuke Him, saying, "Far be it from you, Lord; this shall not happen to You!" But He [Jesus] turned and said to Peter, "Get behind me, Satan! You are an offense to Me, for you are not mindful of the things of God, but the things of men" (vv. 22-23).

Peter rebuked Jesus out of his zeal and love for Him. He did not want his beloved Master to die. However, he was unaware that his zeal was inspired by Satan himself. The primary reason that Jesus was manifested in the flesh was to die on the cross and take away the sin of mankind.

For this purpose the Son of God was manifested, that He might destroy the works of the devil (1 John 3:8).

And you know that He was manifested to take away our sins, and in Him there is no sin (v. 5).

How did He destroy Satan and take away the sin of the world?

Who Himself [Jesus] bore our sins in His own body on the tree, that we, having died to sins, might live for righteousness (1 Pet. 2:24).

The Bible also declares:

When you were dead in your sins and in the uncircumcision of your sinful nature, God made you alive with Christ. He forgave us all our sins, having canceled the written code, with its regulations, that was against us and that stood opposed to us; he took it away, nailing it to the cross. And having disarmed the powers and authorities

[forces of darkness and Satan] he made a public
spectacle of them, triumphing over them by the
cross (Col. 2:13-15, NIV).

The cross and death of Jesus form the very root of
Christianity or, better said, the only hope for man's freedom. Without Jesus' death and the shedding of His blood,
there is no redemption and remission of sin (Heb. 9:22).

To take away the cross of Calvary is to deny God and the
very nature of God. The cross is God's heartbeat for humanity. Without it, mankind is dead and worthless, doomed to
the very gates of hell. No wonder Satan, through the many
religions and philosophies he has inspired, attacks the cross
of Jesus more than anything else. No, we preach Christ crucified, even though it's foolishness to the intellectuals and a
stumbling block to many religious people (1 Cor. 1:23).

Islam Denies the Deity of Jesus

Islam denies that Jesus is the Son of God. In the Koran,
Sura 9:30 states:

The Jews call "Uzayr* a son of God," and the
Christians call "Christ the Son of God." That is a saying from their mouth; (In this) they but imitate what
the Unbelievers of the old used to say. Allah's curse
be on them: how they are deluded away from the
Truth!

The Koran not only denies the deity of Jesus, it also puts
a curse on all who confess Jesus as Lord: "Allah's curse be
on them" (Sura 9:30). Islam is cursing millions upon millions of people who confess Jesus as their Lord and Savior.

The Bible proclaims the deity of Christ:

---

* This name is only mentioned in Islamic writings. The man's identity is uncertain.

> For in Christ all the fullness of the Deity lives in bodily form (Col. 2:9, NIV).

> He [Jesus] is the image of the invisible God (Col. 1:15).

> The Son is the radiance of God's glory and the exact representation of His being (Heb. 1:3, NIV).

> In the beginning was the Word [Jesus], and the Word was with God, and the Word was God...And the Word became flesh and dwelt among us, and we beheld His glory, the glory as of the only begotten of the Father, full of grace and truth (John 1:1,14).

Jesus could not have done what He came to do unless He was God manifested in the flesh.

> Concerning His Son Jesus Christ our Lord, who was born of the seed of David according to the flesh, and declared to be the Son of God with power according to the Spirit of holiness, by the resurrection from the dead (Rom. 1:3-4).

Jesus was proved to be God through His virgin birth, through His ministry of numerous signs and wonders, through His sinless life, through His powerful words, through His death, and finally He is proved to be the Son of God through His resurrection from the dead.

Islam brings the person of Jesus to a place even lower than Muhammad. In Sura 5:75, it says, "Christ, the son of Mary, was no more than a messenger."

How could Jesus, who even the Koran declares sinless (Sura 19:19), be lower than Muhammad, whose past and future sins the Koran admits (Sura 48:2)?

Which prophet has God ever asked to sit at His right hand? "Sit at My right hand, till I make Your enemies Your footstool" (Heb. 1:13). How could Jesus be only a prophet when David called Him Lord? (Ps. 110:1).

Christ, Only a Prophet?

Every prophet who ever was truly sent by God witnessed of Christ, the Messiah. From Genesis through Revelation, every page of the Old and the New Testament testifies of the character and person of Jesus Christ.

In the book of Genesis, Christ is the offspring of the Woman (3:15) and Shiloh (49:10).

In the book of Numbers He is the Star and the Scepter (Num. 24:17).

Job said that Christ is the Redeemer (Job 19:25).

David called Him Lord (Ps. 110:1) and Shepherd (Ps. 23:1).

Solomon said He is the Rose of Sharon and the Lily of the Valley (Song 2:1).

Isaiah called Jesus the Mighty God, Wonderful Counselor, the Everlasting Father, Prince of Peace (Is. 9:6), the Branch (11:1), Banner to the People (11:10), Arm of the Lord (53:1), Man of Sorrows (v. 3), Leader and Commander (55:4).

Jeremiah said He is called the Lord our righteousness (Jer. 23:6).

Daniel called Him the Ancient of Days (Dan. 7:9), the Anointed One (9:25, NIV).

Haggai referred to Him as the Desire of All Nations (Hag. 2:7).

Zechariah called Him King (Zech. 9:9).

Malachi said He is the Messenger of the Covenant (Mal. 3:1) and Sun of Righteousness (4:2).

In the book of Matthew the Christ is called the Son of David (1:21), Jesus (1:1), Immanuel (1:23), Bridegroom

(9:15), Friend (11:19), Servant (12:18), Son of Man (20:28), Prophet (21:11).

In the book of Mark He is the Holy One (1:24), Brother (6:3).

In the book of Luke Jesus is the Horn of Salvation (1:69), the Dayspring (1:78).

In the book of John Jesus is the Word (1:1), the Lamb of God (1:29), the Christ (1:41), Teacher (3:2), Only Begotten Son (3:16), Living Water (4:10), Savior (4:42), Bread of Life (6:35), Light of the World (8:12), I Am (8:58), the Good Shepherd (10:11), the Resurrection and the Life (11:25), the Way, the Truth and the Life (14:6), the True Vine (15:1), God (20:28).

In the book of Acts Jesus is called the Judge (10:42).

Paul said Jesus is our Passover (1 Cor. 5:7), the Rock (10:4), the Last Adam (15:45), Beloved (Eph. 1:6), Chief Cornerstone (2:20), Head (4:15), Head of the church (5:23), Lord (Phil. 2:11), Image of the Invisible God, Firstborn over all creation (Col. 1:15), All in All (3:11), our Hope (1 Tim. 1:1), Mediator, the Man (2:5), Ransom (2:6), the King of kings (6:15).

The writer of the book of Hebrews says that Jesus is the Heir of all things (1:2), radiance of God's glory, exact representation of His being (1:3, NIV), Captain of Salvation (2:10), Apostle of our Profession (3:1), High Priest (6:20), guarantee of a better covenant (7:22, NIV), Author and Finisher of our faith (12:2).

Peter says Jesus is Christ (1 Pet. 1:1) and the Overseer (2:25).

John declares that Jesus is our Advocate (1 John 2:1), our Atoning Sacrifice (2:2).

In the book of Revelation, John looks into heaven and sees the glory of Jesus. John refers to Jesus as the Almighty (Rev. 1:8), the Living One (1:18, NIV), the Amen, Faithful and True Witness (3:14), Lion of the tribe of Judah (15:5),

Alpha and Omega (22:13), the Root and the Offspring of David, the Bright and Morning Star (22:16).

The Bible says that Jesus is:

> before all things, and in Him all things consist. And He is the head of the body, the church, who is the beginning, the firstborn from the dead, that in all things He may have the preeminence (Col. 1:17-18).

Jesus was before any of us who came to be, including Muhammad.

Glory to His wonderful name! Jesus is the First and the Last. He is Alpha and Omega, the Beginning and the End. He is above all creation. By Him all things were created. All things were created through Him and for Him. He is before all things, and in Him all things consist. Jesus is the Son of the living God. This is the truth for every person on earth.

SIX

THE CONFUSION
OF THE KORAN

THE KORAN NOT ONLY DENIES and controverts the foundational truths of the Bible, but it also contains contradictions and errors concerning persons, places and historical and chronological events in the Old and New Testaments.

The Koran contains 114 suras or chapters, starting with the longest sura and ending with the shortest. The order of these suras lacks the historical and chronological order in which these revelations were given to Muhammad during a twenty-two-year period. They were simply put in order of length, starting with the longest and ending with the shortest.

When a revelation came to Muhammad, who is believed to have been illiterate, it was written down by his followers as they heard him recite it. They wrote on whatever they could find to write on — leaves, dried bones, scraps of parchment and so on.

After Muhammad's death these fragments of revelation were collected for the Koran. Since these revelations were given to Muhammad in his native language, Arabic, it is considered essential that every Muslim should read and understand the Koran in Arabic. This is one of the reasons there is very limited knowledge of the Koran among the 60 to 70 percent of the Muslim population who are non-Arabs.

I have more knowledge of the Koran now as a Christian than I ever had as a fanatical Muslim. Of all the Muslims I knew, only a handful had some knowledge of the Koran. Even today when I confront many fanatical Muslims with strange revelations of Muhammad in the Koran, they are unaware these verses are in the book.

To a Muslim, the Koran is Allah's own word to man. It is the most holy book, very revered and respected, even for those who do not understand it or have never read it. This, however, does not change the fact that the Koran as a piece of literature and as a book is nothing but pure confusion and massive repetitions of the same idea.

Many scholars have made comments on the Koran which are very offensive to Muslims. The Scottish scholar Thomas Carlyle once said:

> It is as toilsome reading as I ever undertook, a wearisome, confused jumble, crude, incondite. Nothing but a sense of duty could carry any European through the Koran.[1]

As I have already pointed out, the chronological order of the events mentioned in the Koran is very scrambled and historically inaccurate. It is a grave mistake for one to believe that the God of the Koran is the same God of the Bible.

Many Muslim scholars have attempted to assign a chronological order to the events mentioned in the Koran.

According to the Muslim scholar Ibn-Ishaq, the chronological order for the events mentioned in the Koran is as follows:

> Creation; Adam and Eve; Noah and his issue; Hud; Salih; Abraham; Lot; Job; Shu'ayb; Joseph; Moses; Ezekiel; Elijah; Elisha; Samuel; David; Solomon; Sheba; Isaiah; al-Khidr; Daniel; Hananiah; Azariah; Mishael and Ezra; Alexander; Zecharia and John; the family of Imran and Jesus, son of Mary; the Companion of the Cave; Jonah; the Three Messengers; Samson; George.

Christians would note that many of the so-called prophets in the above list from the Koran are mentioned neither in the Old Testament nor the New Testament. Who are Hud, Salih, Sheba, Shu'ayb, al-Khidr, Alexander, George and the Companion of the Cave? Other than Alexander, the existence of these persons does not even seem to be supported by historical record.

Also, this historical order of the prophets is in pure error. Jonah and Samson are placed after Christ. Ezekiel is placed in the time of the Judges shortly after Joshua. Mary, the mother of Jesus, is confused with Miriam, the sister of Moses and Aaron. Mary is addressed as the sister of Aaron and the daughter of Amram (Sura 3:31-37 and 19:28).

A careful comparison of the Koran with the Bible reveals the many errors recorded in the Koran. The vast differences between the Bible and the Koran, and between the God of the Bible and Allah of the Koran, are undeniable.

On the following pages I will make a comparison between the Bible and verses in the Koran in order to demonstrate how both books address the same stories but in different ways. I have italicized key phrases in both to emphasize major differences.

The Bible and the Koran

BIBLE

KORAN

Noah's Son

So Noah, *with his sons,* his wife, and his sons' wives, went into the ark because of the waters of the flood (Gen. 7:7; see also 7:1-13).

So the ark floated with them on the waves (Towering) like mountains, *and Noah called out to his son, who had separated himself (from the rest):* ...and the waves came between them, and the son was among those overwhelmed in the flood (Sura 11:42-43; see also 11:32-48).

Noah's Ark

Then the ark rested in the seventh month, the seventeenth day of the month, *on the mountains of Ararat* (Gen. 8:4).

Then the word went forth: "O earth! swallow up thy water, and O sky! Withhold (thy rain)!" And the water abated, and the matter was ended. *The ark rested on Mount Judi,* and the word went forth: "Away with those who do wrong!" (Sura 11:44).

Abraham

Then Abram moved his tent, and went and dwelt *by the terebinth trees of Mamre,* which are in Hebron, and built an altar there to the Lord (Gen. 13:18).

O our Lord! I have made some of my offspring to *dwell in a valley without cultivation,** by Thy Sacred House (Ka'bah): in order, O our Lord, that they may establish regular Prayer: So

BIBLE	KORAN
	fill the hearts of some among men with love towards them, and feed them with Fruits: so that they may give thanks (Sura 14:37).
	* This valley is the Meccan valley, where the Muslims believe Abraham built Ka'bah with Ishmael.

Pharaoh

Then the daughter of Pharaoh came down to bathe at the river. And her maidens walked along the riverside; and when she saw the ark among the reeds, she sent her maid to get it (Ex. 2:5).	Then the people of Pharaoh picked him up (from the river): (It was intended) that (Moses) should be to them an adversary and a cause of sorrow: For Pharaoh and Haman and (all) their hosts were men of sin. *The wife of Pharaoh* said: "(Here is) a joy of the eye, for me and for thee: slay him not. It may be that he will be of use to us, or we may adopt him as a son." And they perceived not (what they were doing) (Sura 28:8-9).

Jesus' miracles*

This beginning of signs Jesus did in Cana of Galilee, and manifested His glory; and His disciples	And (appoint him) a messenger to the Children of Israel (with this message): "I have come to you, with

BIBLE

KORAN

believed in Him (John 2:11).

* Here John gives us the record of Jesus' first miracle in Cana of Galilee, changing the water into wine. Compare this with the Koran version concerning the miracles of Jesus.

a Sign from your Lord, in that *I make for you out of clay, as it were, the figure of a bird, and breathe into it, and it becomes a bird by Allah's leave:* And I heal those born blind, and the lepers, and I quicken the dead, by Allah's leave; And I declare to you what ye eat, and what ye store in your houses. Surely therein is a Sign for you if ye did believe (Sura 3:49).

Zechariah's punishment*
But behold, you will be mute and not able to speak *until the day these things take place,* because you did not believe my words which will be fulfilled in their own time (Luke 1:20; see also 1:5-38, 57-80).

* Note that Zechariah was to be mute until the child was born, which was the entire period of his wife's pregnancy. Compare this with the Koran version.

(Zakariya) said: "O my Lord! Give me a Sign." "Thy Sign," was the answer, "shall be that thou shalt speak to no man *for three nights,* although thou art not dumb." (Sura 3:41; see also 3:38-41; 19:16-34).

BIBLE   **KORAN**

Crucifixion

Then they crucified Him, and divided His garments, casting lots, that it might be fulfilled which was spoken by the prophet (Matt. 27:35; see also Mark 15:25; Luke 23:33; John 19:18).

That they said (in boast), "We killed Christ Jesus, the son of Mary, the messenger of Allah," but *they killed him not, nor crucified him, but so it was made to appear to them,* and those who differ therein are full of doubts, with no (certain) knowledge, but only conjecture to follow, for *of a surety they killed him not* (Sura 4:157).

Deity of Jesus

And Simon Peter answered and said, *"You are the Christ, the Son of the living God"* (Matt. 16:16; see also John 10:30; 8:19).

The Jews call "Uzayr a son of God," and the Christians call "Christ the Son of God." *That is a saying from their mouth;* (In this) they but imitate what the Unbelievers of old used to say. Allah's curse be on them: how they are deluded away from the Truth! (Sura 9:30).

Authority of Jesus

God, who at various times and in various ways spoke in time past to the fathers by the prophets, has in these last days spoken to us by *His Son, whom He*

Christ, the son of Mary, was no more than a messenger; many were the messengers that passed away before him. His mother was a woman of truth. They had

BIBLE

has appointed heir of all things, through whom also He made the worlds; who being the brightness of His glory and the express image of His person, and upholding all things by the word of His power, when He had by Himself purged our sins, sat down at the right hand of the Majesty on high (Heb. 1:1-3).

KORAN

both to eat their (daily) food. See how Allah doth make his Signs clear to them; Yet see in what ways they are deluded away from the truth (Sura 5:75).

God's nature

For God so loved the world that He gave His only begotten Son, that whosoever believes in Him should not perish but have everlasting life (John 3:16).

Obey Allah and his messenger: But if they turn back, *Allah loveth not those who reject Faith*...As to those who believe and work righteousness, Allah will pay them (in full) their reward: But *Allah loveth not those who do wrong* (Sura 3:32,57).

God's love

But God demonstrates His own love toward us, in that while we were still sinners, Christ died for us (Rom. 5:8).

Fight in the cause of Allah those who fight you, but do not transgress limits; for Allah loveth not transgressors* (Sura 2:190).

* The concept that Allah does not love sinners is repeated twenty-four times in the Koran.

BIBLE   **KORAN**

Wives

Husbands, love your wives, just as Christ also loved the church and gave Himself for her, that He might sanctify and cleanse her with the washing of water by the word, that He might present her to to Himself a glorious church, not having spot or wrinkle or any such thing, but that she should be holy and without blemish. So husbands ought to love their own wives as their own bodies; he who loves his wife loves himself (Eph. 5:25-28).

Men are the protectors and maintainers of women, because Allah has given the one more (strength) than the other, and because they support them from their means. Therefore the righteous women are devoutly obedient, and guard in (the husband's) absence what Allah would have them guard. As to those women on whose part ye fear disloyalty and ill-conduct, *admonish them (first), (next), refuse to share their beds, (and last) beat them (lightly);** but if they return to obedience, seek not against them means (of annoyance): for Allah is Most High, Most Great (above you all) (Sura 4:34).

* The Arabic text, does not include the word *lightly*. It was added by the translator.

Husbands, likewise, *dwell with them with understanding, giving honor to the wife,* as to the weaker vessel, and as being heirs together of the grace of life, that your prayers may not be hindered (1 Pet. 3:7).

*Your wives are as a tilth** unto you so approach your tilth when or how you will;* but do some good act for your souls before hand; and fear Allah, and know that ye are to meet Him (in the Hereafter), and give

BIBLE	KORAN
	(these) good tidings to those who believe (Sura 2:223). * A tilth is a piece of farmland.

Adultery

Woman, where are those accusers of yours? Has no one condemned you? ...Neither do I condemn you; go and sin no more (John 8:10-11; see also 8:2-11).	If adultery is proved for married woman through the testimony of four witnesses, then detain them in their house until death takes them or God appoints for them a way (Sura 4:15).

God's children

Beloved, now we are children of God; and it has not yet been revealed what we shall be, but we know that when He is revealed, we shall be like Him, for we shall see Him as He is (1 John 3:2).	(Both) the Jews and the Christians say: "We are sons of Allah, and His beloved," Say: "Why then doth He punish you for your sins? Nay, ye are but men — of the men He hath created: He forgiveth whom He pleaseth, and he punisheth whom He pleaseth: and to Allah belongeth the dominion of the heavens and the earth, and all that is between: and unto Him is the final goal (of all) (Sura 5:18).

BIBLE   **KORAN**

Heaven

For when they rise from the dead, they neither marry nor are given in marriage, but are like angels in heaven (Mark 12:25).

But give glad tidings to those who believe and work righteousness, that their portion is Gardens, beneath which rivers flow. Every time they are fed with fruits therefrom, they say: "Why, this is what we were fed with before," for they are given things in similitude; and they have therein companions pure (and holy); and they abide therein (forever) (Sura 2:25).

And he showed me a pure *river of water of life,* clear as crystal, proceeding from the throne of God and of the Lamb. In the middle of its street, and on either side of the river, was the tree of life, which bore twelve fruits, each tree yielding its fruit every month. The leaves of the tree were for the healing of the nations. And there shall be no more curse, but the throne of God and of the Lamb shall be in it, and His servants shall serve Him. They shall see His face, and His name shall be on their foreheads (Rev. 22:1-4).

(Here is) a Parable of the Garden which the righteous are promised: In its are rivers of water incorruptible; *rivers of milk of which the taste never changes; rivers of wine, a joy to those who drink; and rivers of honey pure and clear.* In it there are for them all kinds of fruits; and Grace from their Lord. (Can those in such Bliss) be compared to such as shall dwell forever in the Fire, and be given, to drink, boiling water, so that it cuts up their bowels (to pieces)? (Sura 47:15).

The Sin Problem

As you can see, the Koran and the Bible differ greatly. One of the most significant differences is teaching about sin. If you ask a Muslim what will happen to him when he dies, he will answer, "Only God knows!"

Muslims do not have assurance of salvation because Islam does not give them a promise of salvation. As a matter of fact, the word *salvation* is unknown to them.

The Koran, in Sura 13:22-23, says, "Those who avert evil with good theirs shall be the ultimate abode, Gardens of Eden which they shall enter; and those who were good to their parents and wives and their seed."

In other words, the promise of eternal life depends upon good works. They believe that if their good deeds outweigh their bad ones then they might get to heaven. Because they are not sure about the matter, it would be presumptuous for them to say they will have eternal life.

Muslims are very doubtful of the love of Allah toward them. The Koran records twenty-four times that Allah does not love sinners (Sura 2:190ff), but only those who fear him (Sura 3:76). This is the reason Muslims feel so dependent upon their good works. Thus, salvation for sinners does not exist in Islam.

One *hadith* (story about the traditions of Muhammad) tells of a time when Khadijeh, the wife of Muhammad, asked him to forgive her sins. He replied that he was not sure if his sins were forgiven! How could he then forgive her sins? If Muhammad, the highest authority in Islam, was not sure that his sins were forgiven, how then could Muslims have that assurance?

I often ask the following question when I talk with a Muslim: "Are your sins forgiven you?" The usual answer is either, "Only God knows," or "God is merciful." Then I ask again until the answer is no.

Even though the contents of the Koran refer often to Allah's forgiveness, assurance of salvation or of forgiveness of sins cannot be found in the Koran for a Muslim or anybody else. Therefore, not a single Muslim in the world can tell you boldly that his sins are forgiven and that he has eternal life.

Let me give you an example. In Sura 2:158 we are told that those who make the pilgrimage to Mecca will be counted as faultless. I know of many people who have made the pilgrimage to Mecca, including my own brother and sister. Yet they have no assurance that their sins are forgiven, nor are they people you could call faultless.

In another place in the Koran it says, "Men who fast and woman who fast...for them Allah has prepared forgiveness and great reward" (Sura 33:35). I fasted every year for thirty days during the month of Ramadan, yet not a single time did I ever have the assurance of forgiveness for my sins.

Sin Justification

Since there is no such thing as forgiveness of sins in Islam, Muslims justify their sins. True conviction of sin does not exist in Islam.

For instance, a lie can be labeled as a white lie, which is not counted as sin. "As long as my lies can help someone, they are not sin," they reason. Adultery and fornication can be labeled as a temporary marriage (Sura 4:3-34). It has been a common practice for traveling married men to take another woman into a temporary marriage. Muhammad himself had at least twelve wives and two concubines.

Muhammad's adopted son, Zaid, was one of the first to accept the faith of Islam. He was married to Muhammad's cousin, Zainab. She was a beautiful woman to whom

81

Muhammad was attracted. A revelation came to Muhammad from Allah to ask Zaid to divorce his wife "after he had accomplished what he would of her" so that Muhammad could marry her. Fearing Allah, Zaid had no choice but to obey the command of the prophet, divorce his wife and allow her to marry Muhammad (Sura 33:36-38).

A *hadith* is also told about Ali, the successor of Muhammad, the fourth caliphate (according to the Shiite). One day a man came running by while Ali sat on a chair. After the man ran past, Ali moved into another chair. Right away a group of people came searching for the man who had recently passed by Ali. When these people asked Ali if he had seen the man, he replied, "Since I have sat on this chair I have not seen anyone." This story is admired by many Shiites. They count it as a white lie which was told in wisdom. In their opinion, white lies are the lies that help people.

Blind Faith

The majority of Muslims have very little knowledge of Islam. They are not versed in the Koran or in the history of Islam. Their knowledge is based mostly on tales and stories handed down to them by their parents and on what they have learned from social religious gatherings.

My father would often tell us *hadiths* about the life of Muhammad or one of the Shiite imams (pontiffs). Through these tales, Muhammad and the imams are portrayed as extremely kind and super-righteous human beings. Because of these untrue and exaggerated tales, these men are counted sinless and very holy. Many Muslims believe that Muhammad was sinless even though the Koran does not count him sinless (Sura 48:2).

Because of these inflated stories about Muhammad and the imams, a tremendous love and respect has been implanted in the hearts of Muslims toward these leaders and, consequently, toward God. Therefore, to a Muslim, to blaspheme these leaders of Islam is to blaspheme God.

There are two main reasons why Muslims know so little about their holy book, the Koran:

1. The rate of illiteracy among Muslims is very high. In some Muslim countries in Africa and Asia, 75 to 85 percent of the people cannot read or write.

2. Muslims believe the Koran must be read in the Arabic language, which is spoken only by Arab Muslims. It is a foreign language for the majority of Muslims. The twenty-two Arab nations of the world have a total of 140 to 200 million Muslims. Arabs make up only 19 to 20 percent of the Islamic world. Therefore, some 800 million Muslims cannot read, write or speak Arabic.

My personal knowledge of the Koran was very limited because I did not know the Arabic language. Even though I studied Arabic as a foreign language for three years in school, it is not an easy language to learn. I can read, write and partially understand Arabic; however, I do not know enough to understand it fully without translation.

Many Muslims have not read the Koran for themselves since few Muslims are able to read Arabic, even though they have studied the language.

One time I was witnessing to an Arab Muslim and I asked him, as I often do when witnessing to Muslims, "Do you read the Koran? Do you understand it?"

"I cannot understand the Koran," he responded. "The writing is so poetic and majestic that it is beyond my understanding."

"You speak Arabic, don't you?" I asked him, since the Muslims believe the Koran must be read in Arabic.

"Yes, I do," he answered, "But the writing is too beautiful and complex for me to understand."

"Why would God reveal His word so eloquently that it would be too hard to understand?" I questioned him. "Why bother reading it? If it is so hard for you who speak the language of the Koran to understand it, woe to me who doesn't even pronounce my prayers in Arabic correctly," I continued.

That man was not converted at that moment, yet I was able to communicate with him in a way that avoided argument but made him look at the Koran in a new way.

It is very important not to argue with Muslims about the Koran and the Bible. Muslims believe the Bible has been *tahrif,* meaning "altered" or "corrupted." They believe that the Bible is not accurate since Jesus did not write it Himself. Since the Bible contradicts the Koran, they also believe that the Bible has been elaborated on through the years by Christians. They say the Koran is more accurate than the Bible because it is the exact revelation that was given to Muhammad.

If you have some knowledge of the Koran, you can easily win some points in an argument with a Muslim. But, remember that your points will not win their hearts to Christ. Once you get into discussion with a Muslim, you will realize that he cannot quote freely from the Koran. What he may know of the Koran is passed down information.

Thus, the faith of majority of Muslims is based on their social culture rather than the fundamentals of Islam. If the society in which they live is strongly influenced by the laws of Islam, then Muslims are most likely to be the fanatical kind. Other than that, you will find that Muslims are following a tradition of their ancestors and their faith is a blind faith in a religion and a god of whom they know very little.

Knowing about Islam, the Koran and the different Muslim movements provides the foundation needed to begin to understand the Muslim. But this is only a beginning. The next step is reaching the Muslim for Christ.

PART II

REACHING THE MUSLIM WORLD

SEVEN

BIND THE STRONG MAN

REACHING MUSLIMS FOR CHRIST REQUIRES more than a testimony or convincing argument. It requires spiritual warfare.

When I arrive where we are having a crusade, I spend as many as seven hours a day praying before the meeting. We usually have a group of intercessors who pray at least two hours every day. Without offering these prayers there is no way we can accomplish this mighty and challenging task. Jesus said, "Watch therefore, and pray always" (Luke 21:36). Prayer has been, is and will always be the key to revival.

War in the Spirit

We are in a battle between the kingdom of light and the

kingdom of darkness. However, we must remember that our fight is not against Muslims, Hindus, Buddhists or any other people who practice false religions. We wrestle against the principalities and powers that hold these people in bondage.

> For though we walk in the flesh, we do not war according to the flesh. For the weapons of our warfare are not carnal but mighty in God for pulling down strongholds, casting down arguments and every high thing that exalts itself against the knowledge of God, bringing every thought into captivity to the obedience of Christ (2 Cor. 10:3-5).

Paul also writes to the believers in Ephesus:

> For we do not wrestle against flesh and blood, but against principalities, against powers, against the rulers of the darkness of this age, against spiritual hosts of wickedness in the heavenly places (Eph. 6:12).

You may ask, "How do we do this?" Paul continues:

> Praying always with all prayer and supplication in the Spirit, being watchful to this end with all perseverance and supplication for all the saints (v. 18).

It is only through prayer, intercession and binding these forces that we can proclaim freedom for their captives. This is the reason we spend so much time in prayer and intercession.

For example, before I traveled to the countries of Kazakhstan and Kyrgyzstan in the former Soviet Union I prayed for these countries for eight months. I fasted and prayed every week for those two nations. As a result, we had tens of thousands of people, mostly Muslims, saved in our crusades in these two countries.

Our emphasis in prayer is that God will open the door supernaturally for the gospel. We pray that God's power will be manifested in signs and wonders and that the Holy Spirit will convict people of sin.

We bind the spirits of fear, sin, self-justification, hatred, revenge, death, bloodshed, lying and lust; in other words, the pillars of Islam. Then we proclaim freedom for the captives.

Jesus said, "Or how can one enter a strong man's house and plunder his goods, unless he first binds the strong man? And then he will plunder his house" (Matt. 12:29).

Luke gives us a more detailed version of what Jesus said:

> When a strong man, fully armed, guards his own palace, his goods are in peace. But when a stronger than he comes upon him and overcomes him, he takes from him all his armor in which he trusted, and divides his spoil (Luke 11:21-22).

It is a grave mistake to underestimate the enemy. We must realize the potential of the one against whom we are fighting. When Jesus responded to the Pharisees in Luke 11:21, He identified Satan as a strong man. He recognized Satan's strength.

Jesus also recognized that the strong man is fully armed. What is his armor? Fear of death has been one of Satan's greatest armors. Other parts of his armor are condemnation, guilt, deception, sickness, death, hate and bitterness. Because he is armed against humanity, his stronghold is guarded and his goods are in peace. In other words, the people in his bondage whom he has blinded and deceived will continue to be his prisoners as long as Satan is fully armed.

But the story does not end here. Jesus continues with the

word *but*. This means there is more to this story. "But, when a stronger than he..." Oh, hallelujah! Isn't this good news? Our Jesus is stronger than Satan and all the powers of the enemy.

> But when a stronger than he comes upon [attacks] him and overcomes him, [Jesus] takes from him [Satan] all his armor [fear, condemnation, deception] in which he trusted, and divides his spoils (v. 22).

Let's see what Jesus did to the devil and all his armor in which he trusted.

> And you, being dead in your trespasses and the uncircumcision of your flesh, He has made alive together with Him, having forgiven you all trespasses, having wiped out the handwriting of requirements that was against us, which was contrary to us. And He has taken it out of the way, having nailed it to the cross (Col. 2:13-14).

> He has delivered us from the power of darkness and conveyed us into the kingdom of the Son of His love, in whom we have redemption through His blood, the forgiveness of sins (Col. 1:13-14).

> Inasmuch then as the children have partaken of flesh and blood, He Himself likewise shared in the same, that through death He might destroy him who had the power of death, that is, the devil, and release those who through fear of death were all their lifetime subject to bondage (Heb. 2:14-15).

And because of the finished work of Christ, we have been given authority and power over all the powers of the enemy. Jesus said in Luke 10:

> Behold, I give you the authority to trample on serpents and scorpions, and over all the power of the enemy, and nothing shall by any means hurt you (v. 19).

Love the Muslim

We must be stronger than the enemy in order to bind him. Jesus said that someone stronger than him comes upon him. You cannot come upon Satan and bind him and bind the strong man of Islam if you are afraid of Islam or if you are afraid of Muslims. Before you win Muslims to Christ, you must love them the way Jesus loves them because in love, there is no fear. The Bible says that "perfect love casts out fear" (1 John 4:18).

Before you come against the strong man of Islam and before you proclaim freedom for the captives of Islam, you must love Muslims with the love of God, or else you will be defeated.

I believe that this is where the church has missed the mark. I often hear others say that Muslims are hard to win to Christ. Do you know why they are hard to win? Because we have not loved them the way Jesus loves them. We love them out of obligation because Christians are not supposed to hate anybody! This kind of love is a religious love; it is very shallow and has no power to overcome.

It is not hard for the Holy Spirit to convict and convince the Muslims. Nobody is too hard for the Holy Spirit. Is there anything too hard for God? The problem is not *their* hardness, but rather the hardness and unbelief of *our own hearts*.

I believe that we can bind the strong man of Islam and proclaim freedom for millions of Muslims for whom Christ gave His life. Can you believe it, too?

Proclaim Their Freedom

When I heard the gospel for the first time in my life, an awful fear began to grow within me, a doubt, a voice of warning. What if I were wrong? What if Muhammad was not sent by God? These thoughts brought a shiver through my bones. I was afraid of God, afraid of resisting Muhammad, afraid of Islam.

Throughout my years as a practicing Muslim and strong follower of Islam, I had learned a tremendous respect for and fear of Muhammad and God. To reject Muhammad and the religion of Islam was to reject God. To deny God meant the wrath of God, which would result in judgment to the pits of hell.

The history of Islam has shown that a Muslim who converts to Christianity or any other religion will pay a high price, especially those who are raised in strict Muslim homes. At the least, he will lose everything and everyone whom he loves. At the worst, he will lose his life.

During the time my Christian friends witnessed to me, I became very interested in the gospel. The more I became fascinated with the truth of Christianity, the more fear increased in my mind. It grew to such an extent that I became afraid of the dark. I could not sleep in a dark room; I had to have a light on. I had nightmares often, and I woke up in the middle of the night filled with fear.

Even after my conversion, I was not instantly free from the fear of Islam. One night shortly after my conversion I had an encounter with the spirit of fear in my room. I woke up from a nightmare in the middle of the night, but as I opened my eyes, it seemed as though some awful sort of being who was full of darkness was standing over my head. Suddenly, I felt something heavy and dreadful land on my chest.

I realized that I was not dreaming, but that I was confronting demonic forces. I knew the only way to defeat those beings was to rebuke them and call upon the name of Jesus. The Bible says, "At the name of Jesus every knee should bow, of those in heaven, and of those on earth, and of those under the earth" (Phil. 2:10).

I knew that if I rebuked Satan in Jesus' name, he had no choice but to leave. But when I tried to open my mouth, I was unable to speak. My jaw was frozen, and I could not utter a word. I did not give up, though; I kept calling upon the name of Jesus in my mind. It was not long before my jaws were loosened, and I shouted the name of Jesus as loud as I could. The moment Jesus' name was uttered from my mouth, I was set totally free. Glory to His name. Since that time I have not feared Islam.

Muslims need someone to tell them that they are free, that they need not be afraid of Allah any longer, that God loves them and that He is not angry with them. Just as fear binds people to Islam, love will bring them to their heavenly Father. The Bible says, "For you did not receive the spirit of bondage again to fear, but you received the Spirit of adoption by whom we cry out, 'Abba, Father'" (Rom. 8:15). It is the love of God as a Father that exhorts us to worship Him, not a spirit of fear. "For God has not given us a spirit of fear, but of power and of love and of a sound mind" (2 Tim. 1:7).

It is the love of God that draws us near to Him in such a closeness that we can call Him Abba, Father. To know the love of God is to be free from the bondage of sin and fear. "There is no fear in love; but perfect love casts out fear" (1 John 4:18).

There is much fear in Islam because God is not recognized as a loving Father. Once a Muslim has a real taste of the divine love of God the Father, all his fear will vanish, and he will be ready to be introduced to the salvation available for him through Jesus Christ — God the Son.

God's Word tells us that there is power in the name of

Jesus to set the captives free. "Nor is there salvation in any other, for there is no other name under heaven given among men by which we must be saved" (Acts 4:12). I have seen Muslims set free by this power many times.

I took a group of Bible school students from Uppsala in Sweden to the south coast of Spain for two weeks of evangelism. Each morning we went out into the streets to hold a street meeting. We invited the people we met to attend our evening meetings in a Christian cafe where we could talk to them individually.

One night, Tommy, one of the students, brought Mustafa, a young man from North Africa, to talk with me. He had already told Mustafa that it was possible for him to be converted to Christ. We sat around a table in the Christian cafe and talked for several hours with Mustafa. He was very open to the gospel, and was willing to accept Jesus as his Lord and Savior after we explained to him how to receive the life of Jesus.

We prayed the prayer of salvation together. As soon as we were finished, he was knocked down onto the table, slain in the Spirit. I stood up in the cafe and started to preach about the power of the name of Jesus, as I felt the Lord commanding me to do. I prayed for the sick in the name of Jesus, and the Lord healed all who came forward for prayer. There was great joy in that place.

Then I went back to my table to check on my newly converted friend, Mustafa. He still lay with his face on the table. I lifted his head, "How are you doing, Mustafa?" I asked.

He had a look of fear upon his face. "There are snakes everywhere," he answered. "They are crawling all over me."

I knew there were demons actively trying to scare this man from his faith in Jesus. I turned to him and with a firm voice commanded the unclean spirits to leave him in the name of Jesus. As soon as the name Jesus was out of my mouth, Mustafa was thrown to the ground and began crawling around like a snake, unconscious of what he was doing. He pulled at his hair and tried to pull off his socks. He tore his undershirt into pieces as he crawled along on his stomach. We turned him over, and I pulled his shirt open so that his clothing would not twist around his neck and strangle him. He clawed at his body while the demons tortured him, but they would not come out.

I cried out to the Lord, "What shall we do?"

"Let everyone leave the room," the Lord answered.

I asked everyone to leave except my interpreter. People wanted to stay and see what would happen, but I told them they had to leave the room. A miracle could not happen in an atmosphere of unbelief. When everyone had left, I cried out aloud, "In the name of Jesus Christ of Nazareth, the Son of the living God, I command you unclean, foul spirits to leave this man!"

Mustafa mumbled something in French. I asked my interpreter what he was saying. "He says, 'Stop it!'" was the reply.

I cried out again, "I will not stop until you all come out of him and leave him alone." All of the sudden Mustafa started to yawn. He stood up, conscious again. His skin felt very hot. We took him to the men's room, and he threw water all over his body. He said he felt very relaxed as though a heavy weight had been lifted from him.

Since he was still weak, we gave him something to eat and drink. He told me he felt as if he had been washed in perfume. He was extremely happy as he realized what God had just done in his life. We later walked him home.

Jesus provided freedom for this young Moroccan man, Mustafa, two thousand years ago through His death and resurrection, yet Mustafa was not free until someone proclaimed his freedom.

Ambassadors for Christ

The great calling of the church is to proclaim freedom for the captives. When Jesus returned to heaven, He left the church as His ambassador on earth.

The church is the body of Christ, and Christ is the head. In the natural, the body will follow the head. Wherever the head goes, so goes the body. Whatever the head commands, the rest of the body obeys. Jesus said, "As the Father has sent me, I also send you" (John 20:21). Jesus also declared, "Most assuredly, I say to you, he who believes in Me, the works that I do he will do also; and greater works than these he will do, because I go to My Father" (John 14:12).

The Bible declares that we can do the same work that Christ did, and even greater. What did He do that we also can do?

> How God anointed Jesus of Nazareth with the Holy Spirit and with power, who went about doing good and healing all who were oppressed by the devil, for God was with Him (Acts 10:38).

In Luke 4, Jesus declares His works and His mission:

> The Spirit of the Lord is upon Me,
> Because He has anointed Me
> To preach the gospel to the poor;
> He has sent Me to heal the brokenhearted,
> To proclaim liberty to the captives
> And recovery of sight to the blind,
> To set at liberty those who are oppressed;
> To proclaim the acceptable year of the Lord
>   (vv. 18-19).

We can and must proclaim freedom and deliverance for

the captives just as Jesus did. God has anointed us with His Spirit for the same reason.

> Our suffering is from God, who also made us sufficient [capable] as ministers of the new covenant, not of the letter but of the Spirit; for the letter kills, but the Spirit gives life (2 Cor. 3:5-6).

We are the ministers of a covenant whose bylaws are set for the freedom of man; freedom from sin and sickness; freedom from death and judgment; freedom from Satan and the demonic forces; freedom from fear, condemnation, guilt and everything else that separates us from the life of God.

But we are not true servants and ministers of this new covenant if we fail to abide by its bylaws.

> But you are a chosen generation, a royal priesthood, a holy nation, His own special people, that you may proclaim the praises of Him who called you out of darkness into His marvelous light (1 Pet. 2:9).

> I, the Lord, have called You in righteousness,
> And will hold your hand;
> I will keep You and give You as a covenant to the
>   people,
> As a light to the Gentiles,
> To open blind eyes [spiritual],
> To bring out prisoners from the prison,
> Those who sit in darkness from the prison house
>   (Is. 42:6-7).

Therefore, let us boldly proclaim freedom for the captives of Islam.

No Compromise

I recently received a letter from a person in Australia who wrote:

> I am a Christian, and I am currently corresponding with a Muslim. I wrote to him when we first started writing and told him of my belief in Jesus and that it is possible to have a personal relationship with God. He wrote back and told me never to write of such things to him again. I have not since been so blatant in my confession of Christ.
>
> He has continued to write, and we have been writing letters to each other for approximately three years. I have referred to God and prayer and the peace of God in my letters — but have not since been as bold as I first was. I realize my mistake in this and have repented. Now I think it is time to take action again, but I am not sure of how to best go about it. I do not fully understand Muslims.

If what we preach is the only truth, then we must be very bold and confident about it or people will not hear and believe in what we have to say. A compromised message is a reduced and powerless message.

As a young Christian, I learned that there were many different opinions on how to reach a Muslim for Christ. Being a Muslim convert myself, I realized that some of these ideas were so watered down that a person could not find the line between Christianity and Islam.

Some would say, "You cannot tell a Muslim that Jesus is the Son of God because it will offend him." Others would say that you must look like a Muslim if you want to reach them because Paul became all things to all men.

I have heard of people who are so zealous in their efforts

in reaching Muslims that they have become unbiblical. Some of them have gone so far that their witnessing and their message is not good news anymore!

Their preaching is mixed with the lies and teachings of Islam. They claim they have won many Muslims to Christianity, but my question is, "What kind of Christianity?"

It's like the Hindus who believe in Jesus as their Lord. However, they believe that Jesus is a god among many other gods whom they worship. They do not believe in Jesus as the One and only Lord of their lives. Now you may call them Christians, but I don't!

Jesus is not a lord, He is *the Lord*. Not a way, but *the Way* and *the Truth* and *the Life*. Unless you have a faith of this kind, you are not a Christian and a follower of Christ. When I preach to Hindus, I tell them strictly that they are not born-again until they renounce and deny every other god and religion except Jesus.

When as a baby Christian I started to evangelize among Muslims, some so-called experts in Muslim evangelism told me that I shouldn't tell Muslims that Jesus is the Son of God. They told me that Muslims do not understand the concept of the sonship of Jesus. "You may scare them off," they told me.

But they could not get me to follow their unbelief and compromised lifestyle. If Muslims stumble because they hear the truth about Jesus, then let them stumble. If I cannot tell them the truth, then I would rather tell them nothing. Jesus said, "You shall know the truth, and the truth shall make you free" (John 8:32).

Here is where people miss it. They try to win converts rather than true disciples for Jesus. They compromise the Word of God and water down their messages. They come up with methods and gimmicks in order to get Muslims to identify with them and their form of Christianity. Then they say we have won Muslims to Christ!

Please do not misunderstand me. I believe in communicating to people at their level of understanding. I certainly believe in being sensitive to the culture and customs of a people, but none of that makes me compromise the message of the gospel.

For example, it is a sensitive matter for a Western woman to try to witness to a Muslim man unfamiliar with Western culture. Islamic culture forbids openness or friendship between a male and a female in Islamic society. Since witnessing to a person can become a friendship situation, it is a delicate matter for a female to make an effort to win a Muslim male to the Lord. I am sensitive to this matter, and I advise others to be likewise. But being sensitive to people's culture does not mean that we have to shrink the gospel so that it becomes easier for them to swallow.

When Jesus preached the truth of God's Word to His followers, many could not swallow what He taught them. In John 6 Jesus taught that He was the true Bread of Life, that He was the true Manna from heaven, and that if they would eat of Him they would not die like their fathers had died eating manna.

> Your fathers ate the manna in the wilderness, and are dead. This is the bread which comes down from heaven, that one may eat of it and not die. I am the living bread which came down from heaven (John 6:49-51).

Jesus went on talking of His body and His blood and that those who partake of His body and His blood shall have eternal life. Many of His disciples, when they heard this, said, "This is a hard saying; who can understand it?" (v. 60).

When Jesus knew that His disciples murmured about it, He said to them, "Does this offend you?" (v. 61). The Bible says that "from that time many of His disciples went back and walked with Him no more" (v. 66).

Someone has estimated that approximately 70 percent of Jesus' followers turned back and followed Him no more after this teaching. Yet this did not hinder Jesus from preaching the truth as it was, even if it was offensive.

If we are to follow Jesus' example, we must preach the truth of Jesus as He is, whether Muslims like it or not, whether they accept or reject it. We must preach an uncompromised message or else we are not preaching Jesus.

A physician once invited me to visit him. He was concerned about a trip that he was going to take with another group of doctors into a Muslim region. They planned to evangelize and conduct clinics.

He had just returned from a conference on how to reach Muslims. He told me that he was confused about the upcoming trip and the methods that he should use to evangelize Muslims. As he shared his concerns, he made this statement: "I was taught not to tell them to change their religion. We just leave it up to them whether they want to change it or not."

I knew this doctor to be a very bold person about Jesus. He had a strong love for unreached people. I realized that the Christian conference that he had attended had something to do with his confusion. How sad it is when the church preaches more unbelief and more of man's way than faith in God and His ways.

I answered him straight. "If you do not tell them they need Jesus and must repent and renounce their religion, you would be better off not going there. The purpose of your going is to preach the gospel. If you cannot preach the gospel as Jesus told us to, then it is better for you not to preach it at all."

I believe that many have missed the mark by trying to gain favor and friendship with Muslims and avoid confrontation. They have compromised the gospel. Their message does not have a strong foundation. It is like a house built upon sandy ground. Their message does not have the power to convict sinners.

Muslims must know the truth that can set them free. They must know that "there is no other name under heaven given among men by which [they] must be saved" (Acts 4:12). They must know that salvation is found only in Jesus. They must know that without Jesus they are lost and will die in their sins. They must know that Jesus is the only Way, and the only Life and the only Truth.

We must tell them the truth and the whole truth, or we had better tell them nothing. A compromised message can do more harm for the kingdom of God than good. So if you do not have the guts to speak the truth of Jesus, it's better for you just to keep quiet. A compromised message does not have a sharp edge to cut through the marrow into the depth of man's heart.

So speak the truth, the whole truth and nothing but the truth, so help you God.

Avoid Argument

I strongly believe it is a waste of time and energy to compare the Bible to the Koran with a Muslim. The Muslims have a very strong respect and fear of their holy book. No matter how jumbled the Koran is written — historically, chronologically or factually — it is unthinkable for a Muslim to accept the fallacy of the Koran. It is also a strong offense to a Muslim for another person to degrade what they believe to be the most holy thing they possess. Therefore you must avoid getting involved in a comparison argument.

Restrain yourself from putting down what they believe to be most holy. They will lose interest and not listen to you, and they may become angry with you.

A newly converted Iranian man was with us one time as I led street evangelism in the center of the city of Stockholm in Sweden. This new Christian came from a

Muslim background and was very zealous to evangelize Muslims. As I stood talking to someone, I heard somebody scream, "I'll kill you! I'll kill you!" As I looked around to find out what was happening, I saw this Iranian believer arguing with a Muslim man from Pakistan. They were arguing over Muhammad.

I asked the new Christian convert, "What's happening here?"

He answered, "I just told him the truth: Muhammad is dead, and Jesus is alive."

Even though what he had told the man was fact, it was said with an offensive attitude. The Iranian believer was trying to win points in his argument, but he had ridiculed Muhammad, who is revered as highly as God Himself by Muslims.

Turning to the Pakistani man, I laid my hand on his shoulder and lovingly explained to him that although Muhammad's grave is still in Saudi Arabia where Muslims still go to mourn, Jesus' tomb is empty. Jesus is alive. As I continued, he listened carefully to what I had to say. He listened to me because I told him the truth in love, not with an attitude of winning points in the argument.

I often avoid getting into a discussion with a Muslim about Muhammad, the Koran or Islam. Many times after hearing me preach, a Muslim will ask me, "What about Muhammad? What about Islam?"

My response is, "I am not a *mullah* ("Muslim priest"). If you want to know about Islam or Muhammad, you should contact a Muslim preacher." With this I end any further arguments.

However, there are Muslims with serious doubts and much confusion about Islam who are truly seeking the truth. In that case, I do feel free to open up their minds to the truth about Islam. Even so, one has to remember that it is not knowledge of the fallacy of their religion which brings them to conviction of their sins. It is the Holy Spirit. So why should I waste my time and energy talking and arguing about their religion?

Muslims believe that Islam is the final religion, that Muhammad was the last of the prophets and that Muhammad's revelation supersedes all other revelations.

It is said that when Alexandria was conquered in 641, the victorious Arab commander wrote to the Caliph Umar in Medina asking what was to be done with the famous library. He received the reply, "If the books are in accordance with the Koran, they are unnecessary and may be destroyed; if they contradict the Koran, they are dangerous and should certainly be destroyed."[1]

It is no wonder that in Islamic countries the possession of a Bible is counted as breaking the law. The governments of these states do anything to get rid of the Word of God.

I know enough about Islam to embarrass any Muslim scholar. But why should I do that? What is the purpose? Jesus didn't say we should win them through arguments. No, He said we should preach the gospel, heal the sick, cleanse the lepers, raise the dead and cast out demons (Matt. 10:7-8).

Let's avoid arguments and instead preach and manifest the gospel.

EIGHT

WITNESSING TO MUSLIMS

I AM OFTEN ASKED BY Christians, "How can we witness to a Muslim?" or "What are the ways to witness to a Muslim?"

There has been a sense of frustration, almost a feeling of defeat, among many who have made an effort to witness to Muslims. Even though one may find the Muslim people very friendly and even become close friends with some, it has been difficult to communicate the gospel.

Often Christians end up in an exhausting argument with their Muslim friends which has no conclusion. This leads many to believe that Muslims are hard to convert. Let's look at the Muslim people and see why some have shown little interest in listening to and receiving the message of the gospel.

The Needs of Man

We must realize that the heart of man is the same this earth over. Whether people are Muslims, Hindus, Mormons, atheists or humanists; whether they are black or white, Arab or Jew, they all possess the same nature and the same hardness of heart. Certainly, the response of people to the gospel varies from one culture to the other. However, the needs of all people, despite their culture and backgrounds, are the same all over the world — they need to be loved, accepted, forgiven and set free from the bondages that hold them captive.

A vine which is cared for and tended properly will bear the same fruit in California as it does in the hills of Palestine. One plant may take a longer time to produce than the other because of the circumstances and the climate, but both plants are purposed to yield fruits. The heart of man is the same this planet over.

Of course, it is easier for a person in America to respond to the gospel than an Arab in Saudi Arabia. People here in America have heard the gospel many times, and the culture has been based on Christian values. It takes a longer time for a Muslim to be receptive to the gospel which he has never heard. All his life he has been told lies against the Bible, Christians and Christianity. He has been indoctrinated by the laws and regulations of a false religion.

The apostle Paul says that the gospel is "the power of God to salvation" for the Jews and for the Gentiles (Rom. 1:16). God has the answer in the gospel for every need every person has. The gospel is God's treasury upon the face of the earth. It is similar to a Persian bazaar — once you enter the bazaar there is no limit to it. If you have ever shopped in one of these Persian-style shopping malls you understand my comparison. If you are not familiar with the area, you can easily get lost because of its vastness.

Everyone can find something in the bazaar — from the richest person to the poorest, from the sickest to the healthiest, from the weakest to the strongest.

We are all attracted to Jesus through our different needs. Some people need healing, others need love, all need forgiveness, others need acceptance. God met each need through His Word. The gospel gives us faith in Jesus, and that faith brings us to God. The key to man's salvation is in the gospel: "Faith comes by hearing, and hearing by the word of God" (Rom. 10:17).

The key to the gospel is in the person who introduces it to us. You see, God has done all that needs to be done for the redemption of man.

The question is, why are there so many who are not yet saved? It is simply because they do not know, and they have not heard. In other words, "How shall they believe in Him of whom they have not heard? And how shall they hear without a preacher?" (Rom. 10:14).

Muslims Need to Hear the Gospel

God has given us the awesome responsibility and privilege of bringing the glad tidings to the lost and the needy. We must show them where their need is located in the bazaar. We must take their hands and show them the salvation of our God. We must open their eyes and bring them out of prison (Is. 42:7). We must speak the word of faith with authority and power. And we must proclaim their freedom. Oh, hallelujah! What a privilege!

God has equipped us for this task. He has "also made us sufficient [capable] as ministers of the new covenant" (2 Cor. 3:6). We have been made capable of ministering this new life. God has equipped us for the most difficult task. God has appointed enough grace to us so that we may overcome every situation. There is no such thing as an impossible case or a circumstance which is too hard. "Is anything too hard for the Lord?" (Gen. 18:14).

Reaching Muslims and winning them to Christ is easy. We just need to know the way to each man's heart. We must listen to our Helper, the Holy Spirit, and find out the ways in which He touches the heart of each person. We must be led and empowered by Him. The Holy Spirit knows the deepest things of man's heart. He knows our weaknesses, He knows our shortcomings, He knows our thoughts and our needs. He can penetrate through the deepest intention of man's heart and grip it so there is no way out except the way of salvation.

Let us now look at the vital role of this wonderful Person of the trinity in Muslim evangelism.

The Holy Spirit, Our Helper

The work of the Holy Spirit of God is the most vital and the most important part of Muslim evangelism or any other evangelism. Not to recognize His office and His part is to labor in vain. It is of such significance that Jesus said we should not leave town, the place of our dwelling, before we have received His promise, who is the person of the Holy Spirit (Acts 1:4).

Without the Holy Spirit we have no power to be witnesses for Christ.

> But you shall receive power when the Holy Spirit
> has come upon you; and you shall be witnesses to
> Me in Jerusalem, and in all Judea and Samaria,
> and to the end of the earth (Acts 1:8).

When Jesus told His disciples not to leave town unless they were empowered with the Holy Spirit, He knew the stubbornness of the people, the hardness of man's heart and the core of sin that is wrapped around human nature. This is why we need the power, the force, the ability of

God and His anointing in order to show humanity that they need the Savior.

Jesus said to His disciples, "And I will pray the Father, and He will give you another Helper, that He may abide with you forever" (John 14:16). The word *helper* is translated from the Greek word *parakletos*. This word also means "counselor, comforter, advocate."[1] The Holy Spirit has multiple functions in our lives just as Jesus had in the lives of His disciples.

Jesus was the Healer for the sick, the Teacher for the unlearned, the Prophet for the people, the Comforter for the broken, the Provider for the needy, the Helper for the weak and the Savior for the lost. The Holy Spirit is likewise our Comforter, Helper, Teacher, Counselor and Advocate. An advocate is the one who stands by your side and helps you fight your way to victory.

The Holy Spirit is with you to help you lead your Muslim friends to Christ. He will anoint you for the task. He will give you wisdom in how to witness. He will give you the right words at the right time. He will guide you and give you strength. He will help you show the love of Jesus to your Muslim friends. He will bear witness of the Word of God with signs and wonders. He will open the eyes of their understanding so they can see the glory and the authority of Jesus. He will convict them of their sins.

Jesus said, "When He [Holy Spirit] has come, He will convict the world of sin, and of righteousness, and of judgment" (John 16:8). The Holy Spirit is the one who can convict a sinner; we cannot.

I was recently scheduled to preach at a church in Oslo, Norway. I had prepared my sermon in Swedish (which is very similar to Norwegian), but they thought I was planning to speak in English. They had arranged for an interpreter to translate from English into Persian for a large group of Iranian Muslims who were going to come to the meeting.

"I'm sorry," I said. "I cannot preach the sermon in English because I have done all my preparation in Swedish." I could tell they were disappointed. "Don't worry about it," I said. "The Lord will take care of it."

That night I preached in Swedish. A few times I turned to the Iranian visitors and said a few words in Persian to them because there was no interpreter for them. But they could not understand most of the service.

When I gave the altar call, I said in Persian, "All of you, come give your hearts to Jesus." A couple of them got up and came forward. Then a powerful conviction fell on them, and a large group got up and came forward weeping.

One woman was crying loudly, saying, "I don't want money; I don't want healing; I want Jesus. I want peace with God."

People's hearts are only touched this way only through the power of the Holy Spirit.

An American missionary to Iran once told me a story which I believe is one of the reasons people have had little result in winning Muslims to Christ. One day a man came to this missionary and told him that one of his Muslim converts was intoxicated. The missionary humbly answered, "You are right. He is my convert. I am the one who converted him!"

You see, a man can get a person converted, but not convicted. Conversion is a change of religion; conviction is a change of heart.

The Holy Spirit Convicts

Many people today join churches and are very active Christians, yet they are not born again or convicted of their sins. Their hearts are full of hatred, bitterness and unforgiveness. They know *about* Jesus, but they do not know Him. They have not been convicted of their sins and their need of the Savior.

I have seen many so-called converted Muslims who have changed their religion, but not their hearts. Conversion is the work and labor of man, whereas conviction is the work of the Holy Spirit. Without the work of the Holy Spirit of God, all we have is a bunch of converts. Conversion is the work of religion, but conviction is the work of God.

I remember when my dad used to get drunk with his friends and party in our house until late into the night. Often he'd be so drunk he would lose control and start cursing and fighting with my mother. But the time came when he repented of his worldly lifestyle and became a devout Muslim. He stopped partying with his friends and stopped drinking. Even his appearance changed, and he became very religious, like a holy man. He grew a beard, prayed often and read his Koran. He associated with very fanatical Muslims and often attended their meetings, sometimes taking me.

Dad had changed tremendously, but only on the outside. On the inside he was the same man who got drunk and cursed and fought with my mother. The anger, temper, hatred and all the other human qualities were still alive and well in him. You see, he was converted, but not convicted. Islam does not have the power to convict sinners, nor does any other religion. Conviction is impossible without the Holy Spirit.

We need to be dependent totally upon the Holy Spirit in reaching and witnessing to the Muslims. I would rather witness two minutes with the presence and power of the Holy Spirit than two years without Him. If you labor among Muslims without the Holy Spirit, you are laboring in vain.

I know of many people who have labored hard among Muslims with little result. Yet Jesus said, "By this My Father is glorified, that you bear much fruit" (John 15:8). It is the will of God that we win many Muslims into His kingdom.

This is why Jesus commanded the disciples not to leave

Jerusalem until the Holy Spirit had come upon them (Acts 1:8). I believe many of us have left without taking the Holy Spirit and His power with us.

When it comes to evangelism among Muslims, the church's methods come up short. Your technique is power-less. Only God and the power of His Spirit can get the job done. You may get some results with your methods. You may get a few secular Muslims to go to your church and join your activities, but are they really saved and set free? Are they still carrying the things of Islam in their lives? Or are they true disciples of Jesus, filled with His Spirit and set free? If there is the slightest doubt in your heart, you need the Holy Spirit and His power and His anointing.

The Holy Spirit has nothing to do with the charismatics. He is not a property to be owned by any group of people. He is a Person and not a thing. If you do not like the charismatics — fine! You do not need to reject the Holy Spirit and His work.

You need the Holy Spirit whether you are a charismatic or not. He is here to help you, to guide you and to give you strength and power. He wants to acknowledge the word that you preach with signs and miracles. He is where you are, to give you victory in every circumstance. He will fight your case to victory. He is the closest Person you will ever encounter, a Comforter just like Jesus.

Don't grieve Him, and don't quench Him. Love Him; He is so wonderful. Listen to Him and wait upon Him. Remember that He is more eager to see Muslims saved than you are, so let's trust Him with all of our hearts. We need the Holy Spirit.

Do They Understand?

They know nothing, they understand nothing;
their eyes are plastered over so they cannot see,
and their minds closed so they cannot understand
(Is. 44:18, NIV).

In Muslim evangelism you will notice that this description is quite accurate. Since the teachings of Islam and the traditions of Muhammad are so contrary to the teachings of the Bible, the way Muslims think and reason differs much from that of Christians.

The way we as Christians here in the West look at politics, the economy, friendship and many other aspects of life varies greatly from the view of Muslims. This is simply because our religion constitutes our thinking. Thus, our understanding is dissimilar to that of people from other religions. It is extremely imperative, in my opinion, to realize this distinction or else we will not be able to communicate the message of the gospel to the Muslim people.

The Bible says, "With many similar parables Jesus spoke the word to them, as much as they could understand" (Mark 4:33, NIV).

Jesus knew the limitation of people's understanding, even though the majority of His listeners were people versed in the teachings of the Old Testament. Yet He spoke in parables so they could relate to and understand the kingdom of God.

This is where wisdom is needed, because wisdom is the application of knowledge. Without it we will fail to transfer the knowledge of our Savior to those for whom He freely gave His life. If the people fail to understand the words that we preach to them, then those words will take no root in them. Jesus said, "When anyone hears the message about the kingdom and does not understand it, the evil one [Satan] comes and snatches away what was sown in his heart" (Matt. 13:19).

Have you ever heard a preacher speak with a language so sophisticated that you could not understand what he was saying? Were you edified by him? I have heard this kind of preacher, and I tell you he might as well have spoken Chinese, because I couldn't understand the message —

it was too intelligent for me!

In the natural, we communicate the same information to different people in different manners. The way you talk to your child is different from the way you speak to your husband or wife. You may pass on the same information to both of them, but not in the same way, because they are at different levels of understanding.

As we have received the ability to help people understand natural things, God has also enabled us to make people understand spiritual things. Jesus called the crowd to him and said, "Listen and understand" (Matt. 15:10, NIV). The Bible also says that "Jesus opened their minds so they could understand the Scripture" (Luke 24:45, NIV).

A veil covers the minds of people's understanding. It is a veil of unbelief, and it is caused by Satan and the demonic forces. Paul confirmed this:

> But even if our gospel is veiled, it is veiled to those who are perishing, whose minds the god of this age has blinded, who do not believe, lest the light of the gospel of the glory of Christ, who is the image of God, should shine on them (2 Cor. 4:3-4).

When Jesus appeared to Paul (Saul from Tarsus) on the way to Damascus, He told him of the calling of God upon him. Paul tells of this incident before King Agrippa in Acts 26.

> And when we all had fallen to the ground, I heard a voice speaking to me and saying in the Hebrew language, "Saul, Saul, why are you persecuting Me? It is hard for you to kick against the goads." So I said, "Who are You, Lord?" And He said, "I am Jesus, whom you are persecuting. But rise and stand on your feet; for I have appeared to you for this purpose, to make you a minister and a witness both of the things which you have seen and

of the things which I will yet reveal to you. I will deliver you from the Jewish people, as well as from the Gentiles, to whom I now send you, to open their eyes, in order to turn them from darkness to light, and from the power of Satan to God, that they may receive forgiveness of sins and an inheritance among those who are sanctified by faith in Me" (vv. 14-18).

This calling is for Paul and also for us who are witnesses for Christ — "to open their eyes, in order to turn them from darkness to light, and from the power of Satan to God."

Islam is a blinding force. A Muslim can live in a total demeanor of sin, not realizing that he is a sinner.

And in them the prophecy of Isaiah is fulfilled, which says:

"Hearing you will hear and shall not understand,
And seeing you will see and not perceive;
For the hearts of this people has grown dull.
Their ears are hard of hearing,
And their eyes they have closed,
Lest they should see with their eyes and hear with
    their ears,
Lest they should understand with their hearts and
    turn,
So that I should heal them" (Matt. 13:14-15).

You may ask, how can we open their eyes of understanding? Through prayer and through the preaching of the Word. The Bible says, "The entrance of your words gives light; it gives understanding to the simple" (Ps. 119:130). God's Word penetrates through the heart and thoughts of man. It reveals the intentions of their hearts and opens their minds to understand.

NINE

PLANT THE WORD OF GOD IN THEIR HEARTS

THERE IS NO GREATER TOOL the Holy Spirit can use to convict a Muslim than the Word of God. The Bible says, "Faith comes by hearing, and hearing by the word of God" (Rom. 10:17).

My objective in Muslim evangelism is always to bring the Muslims to a place where they can listen to the Word of God.

Many times people ask me to visit their Muslim friends with them. They think I can convince them more than they can just because I come from a Muslim background. But that conception is wrong! As far as I am concerned, only one person can convict man of his sin, whether Muslim, Hindu, Jew or atheist. This is the person of the Holy Spirit.

I do not possess a greater influence upon Muslims because I come from a Muslim background. I may approach them differently, but their faith cannot be based on my experience. Their faith must be grounded on the Word of God.

If you are involved in Muslim evangelism, it is vital that you understand the effect and power of the Word of God on a Muslim.

> For the Word of God is living and powerful, and sharper than any two-edged sword, piercing even to the division of soul and spirit, and of the joints and marrow, and is a discerner of the thoughts and intents of the heart (Heb. 4:12).

It is the Word of God which can pierce all the way to the very depths of man's heart. A divine energy is stored in the Word of God which can create faith. If the Word sinks down in the heart of a person and remains, then that Word will eventually bring forth life regardless of that person's race, religion or background. It is like a seed planted and settled in the ground. It will undoubtedly bring forth its kind. Likewise the Word of God which takes root in a Muslim heart will bring forth fruit.

The Word Is a Seed

The Word of God is like a seed. The seed has a potential for life and growth. You can reap tons of fruits from a small bag of seeds. A huge watermelon is hidden in every watermelon seed, and within that watermelon are hundreds of other seeds. Where did they all come from? From one little seed. Isn't this a miracle?

In the same manner the potential for faith, healing, restoration, forgiveness and life are in God's Word. One may not see the impact of the Word at once, but if that

Word is planted on good ground, it will surely bear fruit. It must, because it has life and energy stored in it. Jesus said that His words were life and spirit (John 6:63).

When I started to read the Bible in my native language, doubts about Islam arose in my heart. Why? "The entrance of Your words gives light" (Ps. 119:130). The more I read the Bible, the more faith arose in my heart toward Jesus. I was convicted that Jesus was the truth, that I was a sinner and that I needed forgiveness and cleansing.

Years after I became a Christian, I preached in Sodermalm Church in Stockholm. After the service an Iranian Muslim man came to me. He acted very hostile and wanted to argue with me. I told him that I did not have the time to argue. But the man was very persistent.

"Well," I responded, "if you want to argue with me, go and read the Bible first. Then come back to me and I may have some time for an argument!" I was finally able to get him off my back. To be honest with you, I just wanted to get rid of the man because I was too tired after my preaching to argue with anyone.

But a few months later when I returned to that church to preach, this fellow showed up again after my preaching. He asked me very kindly if he could help me in any matter.

"Do I know you?" I asked. I did not recognize him.

"I am the one who wanted to argue with you, but you told me to read the Bible first," he explained. "I have read the Bible, and I want you to know that I accepted Jesus as my Lord and have been baptized by the pastor here in the church."

Then I remembered him. What a difference in his countenance! No wonder I did not recognize him. You see, faith comes by hearing the Word of God (Rom. 10:17).

People say that Muslims are hard to convert. Why? It is because a Muslim is like ground that has never been plowed, worked at and turned over. Have you ever tried to grow a vegetable in sandy or stony ground? I have, and I know it is not easy! My wife, who was raised on a farm, tried to tell me, a city boy, that it wouldn't work. I didn't listen to her, but I soon discovered that she was right.

The Muslim world has not been yielding to the gospel because the church has not been working on that kind of ground. The church hasn't plowed, tilled and sowed on the Muslim fields. The only recorded history that we have of church activity in the Muslim world is the Crusades, which certainly didn't introduce people to the love of Christ.

You have to realize that man is in the same state spiritually all over this planet. Human nature is the same the world over. I have traveled and preached in over thirty countries around the world. I have met people from all kinds of cultures living in many different conditions. I have learned that the human heart is the same everywhere. "The heart is deceitful above all things, and desperately wicked; who can know it?" (Jer. 17:9).

As a matter of fact, it is easier to witness to a Muslim than to an indifferent atheist. Many Muslims love God and have a respect for Jesus, whom they believe is one of the prophets. However, an atheist arrogantly rejects the existence of God and thus disregards faith in God.

But most people in the West are not atheists. Even the most radical sinners have been to a church once or twice in their lifetime. They have heard the Word of God. Here in the United States people can listen to twenty-four-hour Christian television and radio. There is a church on every corner of this nation. People in the West have had their ground worked on. Therefore, when they hear and receive the Word, they accept Jesus easier than Muslims do.

It takes longer for a Muslim to respond to the gospel because faith comes by hearing the Word of God, and they haven't heard it. But, once they hear the Word, the Holy Spirit has something to work with in their hearts.

The Spirit Acts Through the Word

The Holy Spirit brings conviction of sin through the Word of God. Jesus said concerning the work of the Holy Spirit that "He will convict the world of sin, and of righteousness, and of judgment" (John 16:8).

The Holy Spirit takes the Word of God and makes it real to the heart of the hearers. He convicts them with the Word. The Word becomes alive to the ear of those who hear it.

David fell into the sin of adultery with the wife of one of his brave soldiers. After David slept with that woman, he plotted against her husband and had him murdered. David was king over Israel and a man after God's heart, yet when Satan knocked at the door, David let him in.

David was not convicted of his wicked act until the day that Nathan, the prophet of God, brought the word of God to him. When David heard the Word, he was convicted and confessed his sin. Psalm 51 is written right after this incident.

> Wash me thoroughly from my iniquity, and cleanse me from my sin. For I acknowledge my transgressions, and my sin is ever before me. Against You, You only, have I sinned, and done this evil in your sight — that You may be found just when You speak, and blameless when You judge (Ps. 51:2-4).

The Holy Spirit convicted David when God's word came to him. Therefore, it is important to preach the Word with the anointing of the Holy Spirit. Because with Him the Word comes alive — full of life and energy.

Bring your Muslim friend to the point of listening to and reading the Word of God. Dr. William Miller, an apostle to the Muslim world who lived half his life in Iran, tells the

121

following story which illustrates the importance of God's Word in reaching Muslims for Christ.

> One day a shoemaker in Meshed, a very religious city in northeastern Iran, brought home for his lunch some cheese which the grocer had wrapped in a page of the New Testament, which he was using for wrapping paper. After eating his lunch he picked up the piece of paper and read the story of the man who hired laborers for his vineyard, and at the end of the day paid all laborers the same wage, whether they had worked twelve hours or one.
>
> The shoemaker liked the story, and the next day went again to the grocery store and bought cheese, asking that it be wrapped "in another page of that book." Finally, on the third day he bought what remained of the New Testament and showed it to his brother. The two of them then went to a missionary, who gave them a complete copy, and also gave them regular instruction in the Word of God. Both men were later baptized and were among the first believers in that city.[1]

It was the reading of the Word that caused faith in Jesus to rise in their hearts. "Having been born again, not of corruptible seed but incorruptible, through the word of God which lives and abides forever" (1 Pet. 1:23).

You may not see the result right away, but be confident that the Word of God will not return void. Just give them as much of the Word as possible. Many times I have seen Muslims come to Jesus just because of one verse that came alive in their hearts.

Satan will do anything to get them away from hearing the Word of God. He comes to snatch away the Word like a bird comes for the seed. That's where your warfare will be.

Pray for the seed that you plant in their heart. Plead the blood of Jesus over the Word that you preached to them.

Prepare yourself through prayer before you start witnessing to a Muslim or anybody else. Just as a seed needs water and light to grow, so does the Word of God. Prayer will prepare their hearts to receive the Word. Rebuke anything that stops them from hearing the Word of God. And remember their faith will come by hearing the Word of God.

Prove the Word With Signs and Wonders

Signs and wonders confirm the Word of God and the message of salvation.

> God also bearing witness both with signs and wonders, with various miracles, and gifts of the Holy Spirit, according to His own will (Heb. 2:4).

"Prove to me that what you say is true!" is the challenge from many Muslims. When you tell them that Jesus is risen from the dead, they want proof. Signs, wonders, miracles and gifts of the Spirit exist to confirm the gospel.

Whenever I conduct a crusade, I ask God to confirm His Word with signs and wonders. I don't do this so the people will be impressed with me. I do it so that their hearts will be opened to the gospel.

You must keep in mind that what you preach to a Muslim contradicts the Koran. You tell them that the Bible is the Word of God, and they tell you that the Koran is the Word of God. You tell them that the Bible says that Jesus is the Son of God, and they tell you that the Koran says that Jesus was only a prophet. You tell them that Jesus is risen from the dead and they tell you that Jesus was never crucified. On and on you may argue against one another. However, if you can prove to them what you say is the truth, then you will get their attention.

I conducted a crusade in the city of Bishkek, the capital of Kyrgyzstan, a former Soviet republic, in March 1993. During my morning prayer the Lord told me, "Tonight, don't be cute with these people. This is a Muslim republic, but I will be with you."

That night I knew what I had to do. I stood up and told the people, "Tonight I am going to prove to you that Muhammad is dead and Jesus is alive. If the blind eyes don't open and the lame don't walk, I am a liar and this book is no good."

After that I preached and prayed for the sick. Two people who came to the meeting were totally blind, one man for twelve years and a woman for four years. Their sight was instantly restored. Several people who were crippled started walking.

Then I asked, "How many of you want to accept the Lord?" Every person I could see raised his or her hand and prayed with me. The power of God opened their hearts to the gospel.

At another crusade in the city of Constantsa, Romania, God's power literally touched thousands of people. On the third day of the crusade, the Lord spoke to me while I was in my hotel room early in the day preparing for the night meeting. He said, "Tonight I will manifest the power of My resurrection" (see Phil. 3:10).

Later that afternoon my interpreter called to say a woman had begged him to send me to visit her sick husband in the local hospital. "They have eight children, and they are desperate for our prayer," my interpreter said. I told him I would go visit the man with our crusade team before the night meeting.

When we entered the hospital room, we found this man lying in bed, unable to walk without the help of his walker. We laid hands on him and commanded him to walk in Jesus' name. He got out of bed and walked out of the room without his walker, instantly healed by the power of God. A friend who was in the room with him was only able to walk with the help of a cane. When he saw his friend walking, he wanted us to pray for him also. As we did, God also healed this man.

There was great joy in that hospital, but we couldn't stay and celebrate. We had to leave for the meeting. The man who was healed decided to follow us to the meeting and testify about the miracle he had just received.

The basketball arena was jammed with people. About nine thousand people were packed like sardines into this place which was built to seat four thousand people. An atmosphere of expectancy and faith was there. People had come to hear the gospel because of the miracles that had been taking place on previous nights.

Before I spoke, the man who was healed at the hospital told people what God had done for him. His testimony got people's attention. Then I preached on the resurrection of Jesus. People were listening intently, and I could feel the presence of the Holy Spirit. The spirit of faith covered me with confidence that God would explode the stronghold of Satan with the power of His Holy Spirit. I felt great boldness in proclaiming this powerful truth of God's Word: "Jesus is alive. He is risen from the dead. Muhammad is dead, but Jesus is alive." I shouted the same words many times with vibrations of faith echoing throughout my entire being.

When you know that God is going to show up, you grow bold and fear does not have the slightest chance. Miracles flow like a river in this kind of atmosphere. When the altar call was given, every person in the arena wanted to get saved. Many Turkish Muslims in that crowd responded to the call of salvation.

After I led the audience in the sinner's prayer, I stood on the platform praying in the language of the Spirit. I waited upon the Holy Spirit to take over the meeting and manifest what I had just preached. I waited in faith that God would fulfill His promise to me earlier in my hotel room: "Tonight I will manifest the power of My resurrection."

Suddenly, as I prayed and rebuked the spirits of sickness and infirmity, there was a cry from the crowd. It was the rejoicing voice of a mother whose young deaf and mute boy had started to hear and talk. Then another deaf and mute person was instantly healed, and the power of God began to explode.

The crowd rejoiced and praised God as one miracle after another took place in that arena. There were healings of all sorts of diseases and sicknesses. Many who were deaf, mute, blind, crippled and lame were being healed everywhere. It was like popcorn popping in the pan as the heat increases. The line of testimonies grew longer and longer. To God be the glory!

Many Muslims who were seeing these miracles taking place broke through the line of ushers we had twenty feet from the platform. They massed around the platform for us to lay our hands on them and pray for them. It was a chaos of no ordinary style. They had witnessed the resurrection power of God at work in the arena that night, and they craved a touch of that power in their own lives. God manifested His miraculous power in an awesome way that night.

> Therefore they stayed there a long time, speaking boldly in the Lord, who was bearing witness to the word of His grace, granting signs and wonders to be done by their hands (Acts 14:3).

By whose hands? The hands of Paul and Barnabas. When they spoke the Word of God boldly, God bore witness to that Word. There was proof of that which they spoke. Signs and wonders are a confirmation that the gospel is the truth.

The early believers "went out and preached everywhere,

the Lord working with them and confirming the word through the accompanying signs" (Mark 16:20). When God is on your side, you will win no matter how the circumstances may look. As long as you are doing your part and believing, God will do His part.

When we do our part, when we go out and preach everywhere, God does His part — working with us and confirming the Word with signs. Signs and wonders make people respond to the cry of their hearts. They shut the voice of unbelief and help people to believe. The Bible says, "Many believed in His name when they saw the signs which He did" (John 2:23).

There are always those people who must see first before they believe. Jesus said, "Unless you people see signs and wonders, you will by no means believe" (John 4:48). Many Muslims will believe when they see the hand of God.

Let us believe God for signs and wonders and the manifestation of the gifts of the Holy Spirit among the Muslim people. God wants to make Himself known among Muslims.

> You have set signs and wonders in the land of Egypt, to this day, and in Israel and among other men; and You have made Yourself a name, as it is this day (Jer. 32:20).

Dreams and Visions

Although Muslims have been deprived of hearing the gospel, it seems that God is abounding supernatural manifestations among them in order to attract them to Christ. This is what Isaiah the prophet said: "For what had not been told them they shall see, and what they had not heard they shall consider" (Is. 52:15).

We have many examples in Scripture of dreams and visions that God used to reveal Himself to His people. Paul (Saul) had a vision of Jesus near the city of Damascus which resulted in his conversion (Acts 9:1-5). Cornelius, a gentile centurion, had a vision of an angel who told him to send for Peter and listen to his message. This resulted in the conversion of Cornelius and his entire family (Acts 10).

I know of many Muslims who have had dreams and visions of Jesus which resulted in their salvation or the edification of their faith in Christ. A few weeks prior to our crusade in Karakul, a city located in eastern Kyrgyzstan near the border of China, God revealed Himself through dreams to two Kyrgiz men, both Muslims. In his dream, each man was told that in the month of May a man would conduct some meetings in the football stadium. Each was told, "Go and listen to the message he brings."

One of them, a young man, found out about the crusade through our coordinator. This young man was hungry for God, and he accepted Jesus during our crusade. He is now one of our key helpers in that city. His family also accepted Jesus eventually.

The other young man also accepted Christ and joined the church that was started after our crusade.

I have had several former Muslims see visions as they were baptized. I baptized one Muslim convert, a young woman, outside of Stockholm, Sweden. When she came up out of the water she just stared into the air as if she were in a trance. I couldn't see what she was focusing on, so I asked her, "What is happening?" She said, "I see the Lord in the water with us, and He is talking to me."

Another time I witnessed to a Muslim from Morocco. He was not convinced that Jesus could wash his sins away. However, he was very interested in seeing me again and talking some more about Jesus.

The next day I met with him again. He told me, "Last night I had a dream! I saw myself drowning in the sea. I cried out to God, and a man came down from heaven who was dressed in white, shining clothes. I could not see the man's face, but he stretched out his hands to save me and pulled me out of the water."

"My friend," I said, "Jesus is the One who pulled you up out of the water. He is showing you that He will pull you out of your sin and save your life."

This man from Morocco was finally able to understand the gospel through the dream and my explanation, and he accepted the Lord into his heart.

It's important to understand that when a Muslim experiences a dream or vision, he takes it very seriously. Muslims do not believe that Allah gives dreams or communicates with people, so when something like that happens to one of them, it is really out of the ordinary. They talk about it all the time.

I know of an Iranian man who was arrested by the Iraqis and put in jail. After three years of torture, he decided to commit suicide. He got ahold of some pills in prison. Just as he was preparing to take the pills and end his life, he heard a voice from heaven tell him, "Call upon the name of Jesus." The voice repeated this message three times. Finally he said, "Jesus."

Later that man told me, "When I said Jesus, something lifted from my heart. I felt lighter."

He threw the pills away and later was released from prison. He traveled to Sweden and lived in a refugee camp. One of the people from our ministry team found him there and told him about the gospel. When he heard the name Jesus, he exclaimed, "I know him! I accepted Him." We discipled him, and he continues to serve the Lord.

The book of Job has a wonderful passage of explanation about the way God uses visions and dreams.

> For God may speak in one way, or in another,
> Yet man does not perceive it.
> In a dream, in a vision of the night,

When deep sleep falls upon men,
While slumbering on their beds,
Then He opens the ears of men,
And seals their instruction.
In order to turn man from his deed,
And conceal pride from man,
He keeps back his soul from the Pit,
And his life from perishing by the sword (33:14-18).

Many people have been saved from the pit through dreams and visions. If I could tell about them all, it would fill a book.

Pray and believe God for the supernatural manifestations among the Muslim people. Joel prophesied:

And it shall come to pass afterward
That I will pour out My spirit on all flesh;
Your sons and your daughters shall prophesy,
Your old men shall dream dreams,
Your young men shall see visions (2:28).

When we sow the Word, the Holy Spirit convicts and God causes the growth. Then we can add the love of God which He puts into our hearts for Muslims.

TEN

THE CONQUERING LOVE OF GOD

THERE IS NO GREATER EXPERIENCE for a Muslim than tasting the agape love of God. To know God as a loving and caring Father is a foreign concept to a Muslim. Muslims have never felt nor experienced the love of God in a personal way.

Muslims know God as an awesome, all powerful deity who cannot be approached by men. They fear Him and His wrath.

This is why they have such tremendous respect for their prophets and imams. It is only through prophets and imams that they can approach God. It is a common ritual for Muslims, especially among Shiites, to visit the grave of a dead imam or prophet to pray for them to appeal to Allah on their behalf.

131

To know God and to know His Son Jesus is to experience His love, for the Bible says that "God is love" (1 John 4:8). Love is God's nature and the very substance of His being. Our God says, "I am the Lord, I do not change" (Mal. 3:6). This means His nature of love is unchangeable. Thus, His love is from eternity to eternity.

Man's Love and God's Love

God's kind of love (agape) is divine. It is different from any expression of the love of man. Man's love has a very selfish and egotistic nature. It is selfish because it seeks to love that which is profitable and good for the ego.

Man's love is conditional. It is based on a temporary position and situation. The same people who vowed to love each other until death do they part tear each other apart in the divorce courts.

Man's kind of love is changeable. The same people who shouted, "Hosanna," when Jesus entered Jerusalem on the donkey also shouted, "Crucify Him," a few days later.

Man's kind of love is not based on the truth, but on an emotional concept. At the most, we love those who are in agreement with us or who have things in common with us. The very foundation of twentieth-century love relationships is based on what people have in common with each other. It is counted as foolish to fall in love with someone with whom you have nothing in common.

Man's kind of love is also limited. It goes only to a certain limit; further than that, it is impossible for human nature to love. It is impossible for a natural man to love those who willfully do him wrong.

But God's love is pure, holy, unchangeable, unconditional and boundless. God's love is an impartial love, available at all times for any and every person on the face of the earth. He loves you in spite of your condition or position, whether you are a loser or a winner, rich or poor, black or white, a somebody or a nobody.

God's love is not based on who we are, but on who He is. It is unchangeable because He is unchangeable. God does not love a Christian more than He loves a Muslim or an atheist. God's love is based on the truth because He is the truth. There is no shadow or wavering in Him or His love (James 1:17). God does not love us by chance — He loves us by choice.

God's love is a sacrificial love. He gave the best He had for us so we can have the best He has.

> For God so loved the world that He gave His only
> begotten Son, that whoever believes in Him should
> not perish but have everlasting life (John 3:16).

He did not give in order to gain back. I believe that God would have sent Jesus to die for mankind even if He knew that man would never respond to His love. God's love would prepare salvation regardless of what we did.

There is no limitation, no boundary to the love of God. He loves those who hate Him as much as He loves those who love Him. The Bible says, "But God demonstrates His own love toward us, in that while we were still sinners, Christ died for us" (Rom. 5:8). While we were His enemies, while we shouted, "Crucify Him," while we were deep down in the dirt and dust of sin and unbelief, He died for us. That is agape love — God's kind of love.

Very seldom will you find somebody who is willing to give his life in order to save another. Even if this is the case, it will usually be for a close friend or for family — not for an enemy. Nobody would lay his life down for his enemy. Man is incapable of having that kind of love. But "God is love" (1 John 4:8). He does not produce love and compassion — He *is* love and compassion.

Man is the object of God's love (Ps. 8:4-6; Eph. 3:17-19). His love is necessary for our wholeness. Man is incomplete without the love of God. This is the very reason there are so many flaws in the human soul — so much rejection, self-pity, resentment; so many inferiority complexes and feelings of unworthiness. It is the lack of knowing and experiencing the love of God that has caused man to be incomplete and defective. Our ignorance of God's love was caused by sin. Sin separated man from God, causing a great gap in our knowledge of the nature and character of God.

Man would do anything to get a touch of that love if he knew of its existence. To know and experience God's love is better than life itself because it is in the love of God that man finds his life. To experience that kind of love is to experience the joy of life. Man is miserable without God's love.

When Muslims Taste Love

How wonderful it is when a Muslim gets a taste of God's love. Often when Muslims come to Jesus, they are ready to sacrifice everything they have for Him. They will leave their families, their homes, their backgrounds and their culture just to follow Jesus. Many of them have even given their lives for following Jesus. Why? Because they have tasted the honey! They have tasted God and experienced His love through Jesus.

> By this we know love [God's], because He [Jesus]
> laid down His life for us (1 John 3:16).

As a Muslim I used to make an eighteen-hour pilgrimage to the shrine of a dead imam. I believed that somehow through this dead imam I could draw near to God whom I did not know, but loved and feared. I prayed five times daily; I fasted for thirty consecutive days annually. This was the traditional Muslim fast where no food or drink is taken during daylight hours.

I kept the laws and traditions of Islam so that I would be accepted by God — not loved by God, because in Islam that concept is unknown — just to be accepted by Him. I longed to please God, but with all of that effort I did not experience the presence of God in my life one single time! Not even once!

It was only when I called upon Jesus that I could feel Him and the warmth of God's love, that I could know Him as my Father.

It is in the heart of our heavenly Father to manifest His love to all mankind — to the blacks as well as the whites, to the Jews as well as the Arabs, to the poor as well as the rich, to the evil man as well as the righteous man. God "desires all men to be saved and to come to the knowledge of the truth" (1 Tim. 2:4).

God needs earthly vessels to show His love to lost humanity. God uses His children as channels of His love. The Bible says that "the love of God [agape love] has been poured out in our hearts by the Holy Spirit who was given to us" (Rom. 5:5).

God's kind of love is in us who believe in His Son, Jesus. It is there for us to love others with just as He does. It is there for us to manifest to Muslims, Buddhists and Hindus. Let them have a taste of it.

It was this love shown to me by the Christians who gave me the gospel that drew me to Jesus. It was pure, holy and without any deception or flaws. I was always greatly loved by my family and friends. But the love that I experienced from those believers was totally different. It was unlike any other love I'd ever known in my life. It convicted me. It made me see the real me. It was like a spotlight shining deep into my being.

This is the love Zacchaeus, the chief tax collector in Jericho, experienced when he met Jesus (Luke 19:1-10). Zacchaeus was very unpopular among the people in his community because he was a tax collector. Most likely he was constantly cursed and rejected by people, especially those from whom he collected taxes.

Even though Zacchaeus was rejected by men, he was loved by Jesus. Jesus could have chosen to visit the home of any rich man or highly esteemed religious leader in Jericho. Yet He chose to be with the most unwanted.

Zacchaeus received Jesus with great joy, ordering a great feast for Jesus in his house. When he spent time with Jesus and felt His love and mercy, Zacchaeus could not continue in his ungodly lifestyle any longer. He was convicted of his sins, and he repented in the very presence of Jesus. The love of Jesus conquered sin. Oh, how wonderful is Jesus!

Whenever I minister to a Muslim one-on-one, I show him the love of God. Love and patience are two of the most important characteristics you must have when ministering to Muslims individually. When you minister to a large group in a crusade, it is different. You need to show them the power of God because it is impossible to demonstrate love and patience in that setting and time frame.

From 1983 to 1985, I ministered among Iranian refugees in Spain one-on-one. During that time I spent countless hours with those wonderful people. I either visited them in their homes or invited them to my place. They often shared their meals with me. They have wonderful food! I listened to their stories till late into the nights. Many nights they found a place on their couches for me to stay overnight. They became like families to me. I loved on them not to get them saved, but just because God loved them. That's the kind of love a Muslim needs to receive from us.

The love of God overcomes any barrier. It is so vast and so broad; it does not have any limitation. Oh, that we could understand it and live it.

For this reason I bow my knees...that Christ may

dwell in your hearts through faith; that you, being rooted and grounded in love, may be able to comprehend with all the saints what is the width and length and depth and height — to know the love of Christ which passes knowledge; that you may be filled with all the fullness of God (Eph. 3:14,17-19).

His love is like the gentle breeze, like a warm sunshine on a cold day. It is like the spring rain, refreshing the soul of man. His love is deeper than the deepest ocean, wider than the skies and brighter than the brightest star.

Let the love of God go out from you to your Muslim friends. It has the power to overcome any religious spirit. Let them taste God as He is.

Remember that you have the anointing to be a representative and ambassador of Christ. God will use you to show them His love, His forgiveness, His mercy and His compassion.

You are a living New Testament before Muslims. What they see in you is what they perceive of Jesus. You are a Christian — a Christ-like person. As Jesus was, so are you in this world. Shine Jesus and the love of God. You have it in you.

It is very simple: If you can love them, you can win them.

Love is a conqueror because God is love, and there is no resistance in the human nature against receiving the love of God.

PART III

THE CHURCH RISES UP
TO THE CALL

ELEVEN

GOD'S PLAN FOR THE NATIONS

GOD HAS A PLAN FOR each of the three major groups of people on the earth: 1) the church, 2) the gentile nations, and 3) the Jewish people. These three plans must be fulfilled before the end of the time.

The Church

The church is the bride of Christ. "Let us be glad and rejoice and give Him glory, for the marriage of the Lamb has come, and His wife has made herself ready. And to her it was granted to be arrayed in fine linen, clean and bright, for the fine linen is the righteous acts of the saints" (Rev. 19:7-8).

The church is the means that God will use to fulfill His plan for the nations, as I'll describe later in this chapter.

The Gentile Nations

The gentile nations are all the people outside the Jewish race. No Bible prophet speaks as clearly as Isaiah does concerning the plan of God for the nations. The following verses are a few among many promises that God has for the gentile nations.

> Here is my servant, whom I uphold, my chosen
>   one in whom I delight;
> I will put my Spirit on him and he will bring jus-
>   tice to the nations (Is. 42:1, NIV).

> The Lord will lay bare his holy arm in the sight of
>   all the nations,
> and all the ends of the earth will see the salvation
>   of our God (Is. 52:10, NIV).

> So will he sprinkle many nations, and kings will
>   shut their mouths because of him.
> For what they were not told, they will see, and
>   what they have not heard, they will understand
>   (Is. 52:15, NIV).

> "I will set a sign among them, and I will send some
> of those who survive to the nations — to Tarshish,
> to the Libyans and Lydians (famous as archers), to
> Tubal and Greece, and to the distant islands that
> have not heard of my fame or seen my glory.
> They will proclaim my glory among the nations.
> And they will bring all your brothers, from all the
> nations, to my holy mountain in Jerusalem as an
> offering to the Lord — on horses, in chariots and

wagons, and on mules and camels," says the Lord. "They will bring them, as the Israelites bring their grain offerings, to the temple of the Lord in ceremonially clean vessels" (Is. 66:19-20, NIV).

It is in the purpose and plan of God that all people hear the gospel and many come to know Him.

The Jewish People

Paul tells us in Romans 11:

> For I do not desire, brethren, that you should be ignorant of this mystery, lest you should be wise in your own opinion, that blindness in part has happened to Israel until the fullness of the Gentiles has come in. And so all Israel will be saved, as it is written:

> The Deliverer will come out of Zion,
> And He will turn away ungodliness from Jacob
> (vv. 25-26).

There is actually a spiritual blindness upon the Jewish people, the people of God. They have very little revelation knowledge of Scripture. They may have the book knowledge, but they lack the revelation knowledge. In 2 Corinthians, Paul tells us that there is a veil upon the hearts of his people, the Jews.

> But their minds were blinded. For until this day the same veil remains unlifted in the reading of the Old Testament, because the veil is taken away in Christ...Nevertheless when one turns to the Lord, the veil is taken away (3:14,16).

A Messianic Jew once told me that when she accepted

Jesus as her Messiah, she had a vision of a veil being removed from her eyes. She could then understand the Bible.

One day God will remove blindness (unbelief) from the Jewish people. But that day must wait until the fullness of the gentiles has come in. I truly believe that we are not far from that day.

The Church Is the Key

A careful look at Scripture will reveal that these three faces of God's plan are integrated — one is dependent upon the other.

The plan of God for the nations cannot be totally fulfilled without the church. The church is the key to the end-time world revival. I do not believe God would cause a great awakening in the world without first reviving His church. The church must rise first; then she can wake up the world.

Once the church has made herself ready, she will be able to fulfill the plan of God for the nations. When the church has reached the unreached and proclaimed the gospel to the ends of the earth, the time of the fullness of the gentiles will come in. Then God will take away the unbelief from Jacob and save the entire Jewish nation.

Lift up your eyes and look into the horizon of God's plan for mankind for these last hours. The final chapter of the history of the human race will soon be written.

> And this gospel of the kingdom will be preached in all the world as a witness to all the nations [the people groups], and then the end will come (Matt. 24:14).

This commission is not a choice for the church — it is a mandate. For the church to survive these days, she must be in the plan of God, in the very center of the will of God.

There, and only there, God will be with her. There she will find the protection, blessings, revelation knowledge, fresh anointing and manifestation of the power of the Spirit of God.

When the Pharisees came to John the Baptist and asked him who he was and what he wanted, John answered, "I am the voice" (John 1:23). If the Pharisees were here today to ask the same questions, the most probable answer would be, I am a pastor, or evangelist, or businessman, or homemaker or student.

John was aware that he was more than an evangelist or businessman. He was a voice — that is why he was born. Being a voice wasn't his career; it was his life.

Fulfilling the Great Commission must become a lifestyle for us, not merely an addition to our already busy schedules.

The Muslim World

Nearly one billion people today confess to being Muslims. As I noted earlier, next to Christianity, Islam is the most rapidly expanding religion on earth. With an estimated thirty-eight hundred unreached people groups following Islam, Muslims remain among the most unreached groups of people in our world today.

Islam stretches its wings from North Africa into the Middle East and onward to Asia. It covers North African countries; twenty-two Arab nations; the southern independent republics of the CIS (the former Soviet Union); Turkey, Iran, India, Pakistan, Bangladesh, Afghanistan; some parts of China; Malaysia; and Indonesia, which actually is the most Islamized country in the world with an estimated 140 million Muslims.

The majority of the above nations are located in the 10/40 Window, so named because its location is between the 10th and 40th parallel lines on the globe. More than 90 percent of the world's unevangelized peoples dwell within the boundaries of this region. The dominant religion of this region is Islam. Politically, economically and spiritually, this region of the globe has had a more dominant influence on our world than any other.

Despite being in such an important geographical position and influence, this part of the world remains almost completely untouched by the power of the gospel. Muslims are unreached because the church has not put much effort in reaching this vast harvest of souls.

The only instance where the church as a whole touched the Muslim world was the shameful history of the crusades (950–1350). Crusaders raged a holy war, commanded and blessed by the church, and massacred millions of Muslims. They made an effort to establish the kingdom of God on earth by worldly methods — methods which the New Testament declares to be in enmity with the gospel. As Augustine might have put it, "It was the employment of the instruments of the earthly city to further the City of God."[1]

Even though today's Christianity is not that of the medieval ages, our attitudes toward Muslims have not changed much. Muslims remain unreached even in this age of information and knowledge.

Difficult Questions

Why do churches spend billions of dollars in conferences and seminars, feeding the fed ones and blessing the blessed ones, while 80 percent of missionaries return home due to the lack of funds?

We must check our priorities.

Why do we have more Christian materials in this nation — teaching books, cassettes, videos, twenty-four-hour Christian TV, radio and magazines — than in any other part of the world? The number of Bible translations available in the United States is greater than the number of Christian books that can be found in some Muslim countries. Yet in spite of all its pampering, Christianity in America remains the same. With all the knowledge and faith we have collected, we have not had an impact on a single Muslim nation. Not even one! We have been entrapped by the mind of humanism, self-indulgence and apathy.

Beloved, what is our goal? What are we here for? What are we fighting for? What are we living for? Do you think Jesus gave His life on the cross so that we could become pastors and evangelists? Did He die only to give us a career, a ministry, a good house, a car and good friends? What is the church for? Are we here to make a better utopia? Is our hope only in this world?

Why is only 0.01 percent of all Christian income spent on the unevangelized world?[2] Why is 96 percent of all Christian finances spent in the United States on only 5 percent of the world's population? Why does the United States have approximately one full-time Christian worker for every 230 people, yet those who have never heard the gospel have only one worker for every 450,000 people? Why is it easier to raise funds for ministry in the United States than for unreached areas of the world? Does God love Americans more than the other people of the world? Why do 2.2 billion people, including twelve thousand unreached people groups, know nothing about Jesus yet?

When God opened the doors of former Soviet Union's southern republics, a dwelling place for fifty million Muslims, I wrote to forty churches across America asking for support for our crusades. Only one pastor responded with a check for twenty-five dollars. I wish the rest would have at least sent me a letter of rejection.

During a three-year period (1990–1993), the doors to these republics were wide open for the gospel. After 1993, Islam became the dominant religion in these republics, and one state after another, except Kazakhstan, shut the doors to mission works. I had six crusades scheduled before 1993 that had to be canceled due to the lack of funds. I was only able to do four crusades and some church planting. We must check our priorities.

The declaration of Jesus in Matthew 24:14, "This gospel of the kingdom will be preached in all the world as a witness to all the nations [people groups]," is not an option for the church. It is His commandment.

A Christianity that doesn't reach the unreached and touch the untouched, a Christianity that doesn't burn to tell the story of Jesus, a Christianity that doesn't have compassion for the lost and the needy, is a Christianity that hasn't understood the message of the cross. As our German brother Reinhard Bonnke puts it, "We are a lifeboat, not a cruise ship."

TWELVE

NO FEAR IN FAITH

Some SAY THE DOORS TO Islamic countries are closed. But the Bible says, "I have set before you an open door, and no one can shut it" (Rev. 3:8). Jesus opened the door and no man, no human being or any spirit being, can shut it.

If the doors to the Muslim world are closed, it's simply because we the church have not knocked. We have feared Islam and its fundamentalists.

Fear Limits Faith

The purpose of fear is to control the measure of faith — not to destroy it. Fear causes compromise, and compromise decreases the strength and power of faith. Faith is based on the truth. But compromise concedes to that which is not

148

the truth, becoming a combination of truth and lies. Thus, one who fears is trapped in the snare of compromise where faith cannot function in its full strength.

Goliath was undefeated for forty days and forty nights because David was not there to hear him growling. When a lion roars in the jungle, all animals fear it and stay quiet or run away. There is only one other animal who can roar back — another lion who is stronger than the first one.

When communism roared there was a cold sweat on the back of every capitalist. No man ever dreamed that communism could fall so flat on its face, not even those seated in the White House. But when God said, "Open," every communist door opened, one after the other.

I do not care how forceful Islam is in displaying its ideology. I don't care how grim, ruthless and merciless the authorities are in their coming against the church of the living God in some of these Islamic countries. I do not care how fanatical, how blinded some of these Muslims can be. I do not care how much terrorism sponsored by some of these Islamic nations we encounter. The fact is that Islam is growling and roaring throughout the world, and there is only one force that can put a stop to that spirit — the church of Jesus Christ.

Let's roar back with the power and fire of the Holy Spirit of God. Let's pray for boldness and the manifestation of signs and wonders. Let's believe God for the fall of Islam. Let's believe God for a mighty outpouring of God's Spirit in the Muslim world. Let us cast out the spirit of fear and instead believe God for a mighty revival among Muslims. For with God all things are possible.

Pray for Boldness

To be bold is to stand firmly and confidently, without compromise, despite opposition and adversity. Boldness is

149

needed where opposition has created fear.

After Peter and John came down from the upper room experience of being filled with the Holy Spirit, they preached in the name of Jesus right in the center of a city-wide religious gathering of the Jews. Where did their boldness come from? Their boldness arose from the miracle of healing that had preceded their sermon.

As Peter and John walked together to the temple that morning, they were met by a man sitting at the gate of the temple. This beggar had been lame for forty years — since his birth. Catch the excitement of that miracle moment:

> A certain man lame from his mother's womb...seeing Peter and John about to go into the temple, asked for alms...Then Peter said, "Silver and gold I do not have, but what I do have I give you: In the name of Jesus Christ of Nazareth, rise up and walk." And he took him by the right hand and lifted him up, and immediately his feet and ankle bones received strength. So he, leaping up, stood and walked and entered the temple with them — walking, leaping, and praising God (Acts 3:2-3,6-8).

This man's healing and the bold preaching of Peter and John had a profound effect on the gathering of Jews:

> Many of those who heard the word believed; and the number of the men came to be about five thousand (Acts 4:4).

When the Jews saw that five thousand men believed because of the miracle at the gate of the temple and the preaching in the name of Jesus, they suddenly realized what that name could do to their kingdom. They decided to throw the two preachers into jail overnight.

The next morning Peter and John stood before the great

Sanhedrin, the gathering of the religious rulers, elders and scribes in Jerusalem. This is what they were told:

> They called them [Peter and John] and com-manded them not to speak at all nor teach in the name of Jesus (Acts 4:18).

Notice that the Jews did not command Peter and John not to speak or teach. They commanded them not to speak and teach in Jesus' name. In other words, preach, pray, teach and do whatever you wish, but don't do it under the banner of Jesus.

Why? Because they knew that His name caused the blind to see, the deaf to hear and the lame to walk. Satan knew that salvation and redemption take place by preaching and teaching in the name of Jesus.

> Nor is there salvation in any other, for there is no other name under heaven given among men by which we must be saved (Acts 4:12).

The religious leaders tried to create fear in their hearts through their threats in order to get them to stop speaking in that name. I believe the Sanhedrin succeeded in creating an atmosphere of intimidation and fear, for the disciples took their threats seriously. But they did not allow that fear to stay in their hearts and get rooted; instead they prayed for boldness.

> Now, Lord, look on their threats, and grant to Your servants that with all boldness they may speak Your word, by stretching out Your hand to heal, and that signs and wonders may be done through the name of Your holy Servant Jesus (Acts 4:29-30).

They realized that they needed boldness to speak the Word of God without compromise. They knew if they compromised the Word of God, they would not see the power of God manifested.

I wonder how many preachers of the gospel are bound by fear, the threats of Satan and the religious world?

Fear has rendered many churches and preachers powerless. They are afraid of persecution or afraid of losing their status or salaries. They are afraid of rejection or afraid of losing what they have worked for all their lives. They preach the gospel, but with compromise. They are powerless proclaimers of the gospel of Jesus Christ. Their faith is paralyzed. It is not so much that they do not have faith; it's just that fear has paralyzed their God-given faith.

Make a Stand of Faith

Satan wants to intimidate us so that we dare not believe God for mighty things. He knows that faith in the name of Jesus can accomplish mighty things for God. Satan is not so much after us as he is after trying to get rid of our faith. We are not a threat to him and his kingdom — it is our faith that overcomes him.

> And this is the victory that has overcome the world — our faith (1 John 5:4).

Before I was saved I used to get into fights with a lot of guys twice my size. Even though I knew I was not going to knock them out, I was confident that I would do some damage, which was often the case. I did not fear them because of their stature.

When Goliath challenged the army of Israel, not one man was willing to accept his challenge. I believe every man in that army should have been able to defeat Goliath. Even though he stood more than nine feet tall, he was just a man — not a superhero from Mars. The army of Israel carried the name of God; they professed faith in the God of Abraham, Isaac and Jacob.

But the Bible says, "When Saul and all Israel heard the words of the Philistine, Goliath, they were dismayed and greatly afraid" (1 Sam. 17:11).

They had faith to overcome Goliath, but fear had paralyzed their faith and blinded their eyes so that instead of looking at the greatness of Jehovah God, they kept gazing upon the great size of Goliath.

Fear will take you out of the realm of the supernatural and into the natural. But faith will take you out of the natural and into the supernatural. The difference between David and the rest of the Israelites was the difference between faith and fear.

The Israelites looked at the size of the man, Goliath. David gazed at the greatness of God, Jehovah. The Israelites saw themselves as midgets before Goliath. David saw Goliath as a dwarf before Jehovah. David's view was based on the truth.

Goliath was challenging the God of Israel, not only the Israelites. He said, "I defy the armies of Israel" (v. 10). David recognized his defiance of God and responded by comparing Goliath to Jehovah, not himself.

Faith is based on the truth of God and His eternal Word. Faith cannot be based on the perception of the truth. We have no right to demand victory over issues where God's Word does not apply. We get into all sorts of strife, division, divorce and so on, acting contrary to God's Word, and yet we expect God to give us victory. This is how many miss the walk of faith.

David said, "Who is this uncircumcised Philistine, that he should defy the armies of the living God?" (v. 26). The name of God was at stake — not the fame of the Israelites. Do you see the difference? Satan does not care what kind of fame or notoriety we carry or what denomination covers our ministry. Satan is defeated only when we move by faith and act upon God's Word.

Sometimes people try to impress me with the name of the employer or organization for whom they work. I don't care if you work for the most important person on the face of the earth. What I care about, and what causes a concern in heaven, is in whose name and authority you are doing the work of the kingdom. In whom have you put your trust?

David said to Goliath:

> You come to me with a sword, with a spear, and with a javelin. But I come to you in the name of the Lord of hosts, the God of the armies of Israel, whom you have defied (1 Sam. 17:45).

That is faith without fear, dread or compromise.

The Warriors of God

Days of confrontation with the forces of darkness lie ahead. The church will launch an offensive attack on Satan, taking back that which belongs to God and proclaiming freedom for the captives, the oppressed and the poor.

We are living in an age and decade of spiritual materiality. In other words, the spiritual world is becoming as real and tangible to the man of the twentieth century as the physical and material world is.

The activities of demonic forces on earth have increased tremendously in these past few decades. There is an understanding of the reality of these unseen powers even in the secular world. Witchcraft, satanism, occultism, psychic phenomena and involvement in sects have become common practice among many people today. The world is moving toward an era of darkness and obscurity. In 1 Timothy, Paul says:

Now the Spirit expressly says that in latter times some will depart from the faith, giving heed to deceiving spirits and doctrines of demons (4:1).

Satan is increasing his activities on earth because he knows that his time is soon coming to an end. Every action Satan takes through religion and occultism is intended to hinder the plan of God.

In proclaiming freedom for the captives of these dark forces, one will realize the reality of spiritual warfare — a battle not against flesh and blood, but against principalities, powers and the rulers of this dark world (Eph. 6:12).

But Jesus has already won the victory! God has "raised Him from the dead and seated Him...far above all principality and power and might and dominion, and every name that is named, not only in this age but also in that which is to come. And He [God] put all things under His [Jesus] feet" (Eph. 1:20-22).

Jesus is far above the spirits of Islam, Buddhism, Hinduism, occultism or whatever name they may be called. Everything, including Islam, is under His feet.

The Position of the Believer

The Word of God also declares that God has "raised us up together, and made us sit together in heavenly places in Christ Jesus" (Eph. 2:6).

As the body of Christ, we have the same position over these dark forces that Jesus Himself has. We are positioned above all the powers of the enemy. Since we have a position and authority over them, we have dominion over them. We are more than conquerors in Christ Jesus.

But thanks be to God, who gives us the victory through our Lord Jesus Christ (1 Cor. 15:57).

We do not wage war on our own behalf, but on behalf of those who do not yet know Him. We are commissioned to proclaim freedom for the captives and liberty for those who are downtrodden.

Would you engage in a fight that you knew you would lose? If I did not know that Jesus had made me more than a conqueror in Him and that He has seated me in heavenly places together with Himself and positioned me above all the powers of the enemy, then how could I do what I am doing by faith? I couldn't.

Faith without victory is a human effort. A God-given faith has victory, because in God there is no defeat.

I can rebuke a legion of demons and cast them out because I know of the work of Jesus on Calvary, of His resurrection and of His position. Faith in Christ and His death and resurrection gives me confidence and assurance of victory.

Proclaiming freedom for the captives of these dark forces involves us directly in spiritual warfare. I often conduct crusades in cities where occultism and witchcraft are prevalent. During a series of meetings in one Muslim city, I realized that we had walked into a territorial stronghold for Satan and his demonic forces. When I stood before the people in that city and told them to renounce their gods and follow Jesus, I entered head-to-head combat with Satan. This region was infested with witchcraft and demon worship. Each night at our crusade, demons cried out as they came out of people. People testified how they were tortured physically by these demonic forces. Some had even lost their minds.

When I slept in that city, I had nightmares every night. Some nights I could even feel the demonic presence in my room.

If I had not been sure of my spiritual authority and of my position in Christ Jesus, I would not have had the courage to visit that city as a tourist, much less as a preacher and proclaimer of the gospel.

Satan is still the god of this world, and he has many people under his hold. To believe that we will sail through this life without any trials and persecutions is to be as blind as Bartimaeus the beggar before he met Jesus (see Mark 10:46).

We Have a Job to Do

We cannot put our heads in the sand and blind ourselves to the reality that surrounds us in these last days. Satan is rampaging our cities with murder, abortion, crime, child abuse and every evil imaginable. We have a responsibility, a job to do. We are commissioned and endued with power to serve lost humanity.

It was of this very hour that Jesus said:

> And you will hear of wars and rumors of wars. See that you are not troubled; for all these things must come to pass, but the end is not yet. For nation will rise against nation, and kingdom against kingdom. And there will be famines, pestilences, and earthquakes in various places. All these are the beginning of sorrows.
>
> Then they will deliver you up to tribulation and kill you, and you will be hated by all nations for My name's sake. And then many will be offended, will betray one another, and will hate one another (Matt. 24:6-10).

We see that happening in the world today. The news media report such activity in our everyday news. Nations (or ethnic groups) are rising today against one another all over the face of the earth — in Yugoslavia and Albania, in many republics of the former Soviet Union, in Kurdistan, in the Middle East, in many places in Africa, Asia, South

America and even in the ghettos of America. The Rodney King riots and bloodshed in the city of Los Angeles are a good example of this.

During one of my recent crusades in the city of Bishkek, the capital city of Kyrgyzstan, an angry mob of fanatical Muslims attacked the platform screaming *"Allah-o-akbar"* ("Allah is great") right in the middle of my preaching. They were in such a state of anger and revulsion that their countenances changed colors as they screamed. They wanted to kill me.

We were forced to cancel the meeting and leave the crusade arena. In fact, we left the country. But "thanks be to God who always leads us in triumph in Christ" (2 Cor. 2:14). "Yet in all these things we are more than conquerors through Him who loved us" (Rom. 8:37). Hallelujah!

New Wineskins Seeking New Wine

God is raising up a new brand of Christians — new wineskins thirsty for the new wine of the Spirit of God. They have washed their hands and dipped their vestures in the blood of the Lamb. They know who they are, what they want and where they are going. They have pure hearts and pure motives. They are not seeking their own, nor are they building a kingdom or a career. They want only to please their heavenly Father and do His will.

Their will is made of iron. They will not give up until the day that God takes their breath away. They have a fresh anointing unknown to those bound to tradition and religion. These new warriors possess a pure and simple faith to plead the cause of Christ. They love God with all their heart, mind and soul. They do not seek their own glory but they glorify their Master and Savior.

Through faith they reach the unreachable, touch the untouchable and see the invisible. They are a mighty army arrayed for battle. They are aggressively taking by force

what belongs to God. They are like grasshoppers who
invade wherever God sends them. They are the generation
about whom Joel the prophet prophesied:

> A day of darkness and gloominess,
> A day of clouds and thick darkness,
> Like the morning clouds spread over the moun-
> tains.
> A people come, great and strong,
> The like of whom has never been;
> Nor will there ever be any such after them,
> Even for many successive generations.
>
> A fire devours before them,
> And behind them a flame burns;
> The land is like the Garden of Eden before them,
> And behind them a desolate wilderness;
> Surely nothing shall escape them.
> Their appearance is like the appearance of
> horses;
> And like swift steeds, so they run.
> With a noise like chariots
> Over mountaintops they leap,
> Like the noise of a flaming fire that devours the
> stubble,
> Like a strong people set in battle array.
>
> Before them the people writhe in pain;
> All faces are drained of color.
> They run like mighty men,
> They climb the wall like men of war;
> Every one marches in formation,
> And they do not break ranks.
> They do not push one another;
> Every one marches in his own column.
> Though they lunge between the weapons,

They are not cut down.
They run to and fro in the city,
They run on the wall;
They climb into the houses,
They enter at the windows like a thief.

The earth quakes before them,
The heavens tremble;
The sun and moon grow dark,
And the stars diminish their brightness.
The Lord gives voice before His army,
For His camp is very great;
For strong is the One who executes His word.
For the day of the Lord is great and very terrible;
Who can endure it? (Joel 2:2-11).

Joel was not really speaking of Christians — just God's army. These are God's warriors, craving to fight and to win. They are like children of Issachar who have an understanding of the times and know what they ought to do (see 1 Chr. 12:32). They are not confused or misguided because they seek the face of God continuously.

They are in the likeness of David, Joshua, Jehu, Josiah, Josheb-Basshebeth, Eleazar the son of Dodo, Shammah the son of Agee, and many other men of valor who were thirsty to fight and win great battles and victories for God (see 2 Sam. 23:8-9). These warriors do not fear the enemy and his threats. These are people of character and principle; people of great courage who are bold as lions.

These men and women do not hide behind the forms and traditions of religion or seek glory and honor, but seek to honor the One who sent them. They are burdened for dying humanity and have a vision for the salvation of all people. They are builders of a kingdom which will not be destroyed.

Let's be warriors who do not bawl and wail and feel pity

for themselves in the days of adversity, whose attention is not drawn to anything or anybody except Christ Himself. Let's be people after God's own heart.

THIRTEEN

CHALLENGING GIANTS

WHY WAS DAVID THE ONLY one in all Israel who dared to challenge Goliath? He was just a teenage shepherd boy. How was he different from his brothers and the rest of the army of Israel?

> And all the men of Israel [David's three brothers were among these], when they saw the man [Goliath], fled from him and were dreadfully afraid (1 Sam. 17:24).

For forty days and nights this uncircumcised Philistine defied the armies of Israel. Goliath stood more than nine feet tall. His armor weighed 125 pounds. The staff of his spear was like a weaver's beam, and the iron on his spearhead weighed fifteen pounds (1 Sam. 17:4-7). He was an awesome killing machine.

For forty days and nights he intimidated the people of God and challenged the name of God of Israel. Not a single man among that huge army of 210,000 foot soldiers dared to challenge this uncircumcised giant.

But David was not intimidated by Goliath. What was in him that caused this kind of boldness and courage? He had something that the rest of Israel lacked. He tells us the secret in the following verses:

> Moreover David said, "The Lord, who delivered me from the paw of the lion and from the paw of the bear, He will deliver me from the hand of this Philistine" (v. 37).

David knew God. He had trust that God would defend him. This kind of trust comes only when you know God intimately. Faith is not knowledge about God — it is knowing the character of God. David knew God because he fellowshipped with God. As he shepherded his flock, he would meditate day and night upon the law of God (Ps. 1:2). He loved to be in the presence of God. God had anointed David; he was a man after God's own heart (1 Sam. 13:14).

Men of Valor

When David rose to lead the nation of Israel, the men who served him had the same sort of courage and aggressiveness that David possessed. They were also bear and lion killers, just like their master.

> Some Gadites joined David at the stronghold in the wilderness, mighty men of valor, men trained for battle, who could handle shield and spear,

whose faces were like the faces of lions, and were
as swift as gazelles on the mountains (1 Chr. 12:8).

These men had joined with David while he was in hiding
because of Saul's attempt to kill him. They were brave men
of valor, so full of courage and boldness that their faces
were like the faces of lions. Our faces often mirror what we
are within. David's men were filled with courage. They had
tested their courage, and the record of their actions testifies
to their courage.

> These are the names of the mighty men whom
> David had: Josheb-Basshebeth the Tachmonite,
> chief among the captains. He was called Adino
> the Eznite, because he killed eight hundred men
> at one time. And after him was Eleazar the son of
> Dodo, the Ahohite, one of the three mighty men
> with David when they defied the Philistines who
> were gathered there for battle, and the men of
> Israel had retreated. He arose and attacked the
> Philistines until his hand was weary, and his hand
> stuck to the sword. The Lord brought about a
> great victory that day; and the people returned
> after him only to plunder. And after him was
> Shammah the son of Agee the Hararite. The
> Philistines had gathered together into a troop
> where there was a piece of ground full of lentils.
> So the people fled from the Philistines. But he sta-
> tioned himself in the middle of the field, defended
> it, and killed the Philistines. So the Lord brought
> about a great victory (2 Sam. 23:8-12).

These guys are my kind of workers. I have been looking
in different countries for men like these. Give me a hundred men like Eleazar, and we will shake cities with the
power of God. Men who are sold out and committed. Men

with pure hearts and motives. Men without worldly ambitions; men who cannot be bought.

God is raising up men of this caliber from every corner of this earth in these last days. They come from remote places, different countries, backgrounds, colors and languages. But they have one thing in common — a heart after God's heart.

Like David, they will shake and damage the kingdom of darkness. They will move with the power of the Holy Spirit and speak with authority. They have a fresh and dynamic anointing that will destroy every yoke of Satan. They will bring the nations before God; they serve the King of kings and the Lord of lords. He alone will be exalted through their faithfulness and loyalty of heart.

They pray until there is no breath and strength left for them to wail. They go until there is nowhere else to go. They cry until there are no more tears left to shed. They fight until there are no more battles to win. They give until there is nothing more to give. And they believe until there are no more promises to be claimed. They are the Jesus generation, the warriors of light, made in the image of the invisible God.

The glory of God will cover the earth from north to south and from east to west. People will know that God alone is worthy of praise, honor, power and majesty forever and ever. Amen.

The Enemy of Our Souls

From the very beginning of the human race, there has been a spiritual battle for man's soul. Satan has pulled people who are made in the image of God into a dark and eternal pit of damnation.

In Isaiah and also in Ezekiel, we read of the origin of Lucifer ("Day Star") and his fall into becoming Satan ("Adversary").

How you are fallen from heaven,
O Lucifer, son of the morning!
How you are cut down to the ground,
You who weakened the nations!
For you have said in your heart:
"I will ascend into heaven,
I will exalt my throne above the stars of God;
I will also sit on the mount of the congregation
On the farthest sides of the north;
I will ascend above the heights of the clouds,
I will be like the Most High."
Yet you shall be brought down to Sheol,
To the lowest depths of the Pit.

Those who see you will gaze at you,
And consider you, saying:
"Is this the man who made the earth tremble,
Who shook kingdoms,
Who made the world as a wilderness
And destroyed its cities,
Who did not open the house of his prisoners?"
    (Is. 14:12-17).

Son of man, take up lamentation for the king of
Tyre, and say to him, "Thus says the Lord God:

You were the seal of perfection,
Full of wisdom and perfect in beauty.
You were in Eden, the garden of God;
Every precious stone was your covering:
The sardius, topaz, and diamond,
Beryl, onyx, and jasper,
Sapphire, turquoise, and emerald with gold.
The workmanship of your timbrels and pipes
Was prepared for you on the day you were
    created.

You were the anointed cherub who covers;
I established you;
You were on the holy mountain of God;
You walked back and forth in the midst of fiery
    stones.
You were perfect in your ways from the day you
    were created,
Till iniquity was found in you.

By the abundance of your trading
You became filled with violence within,
And you sinned;
Therefore I cast you as a profane thing
Out of the mountain of God;
And I destroyed you, O covering cherub,
From the midst of the fiery stones.

Your heart was lifted up because of your beauty;
You corrupted your wisdom for the sake of your
    splendor;
I cast you to the ground,
I laid you before kings,
That they might gaze at you.

You defiled your sanctuaries
By the multitude of your iniquities,
By the iniquity of your trading;
Therefore I brought fire from your midst;
It devoured you,
And I turned you to ashes upon the earth
In the sight of all who saw you.
All who knew you among the peoples are aston-
    ished at you;
You have become a horror,
And shall be no more forever" (Ez. 28:11-19).

These passages tell us that Lucifer was created a beautiful angel, an anointed cherub. He was the seal of perfection, full of wisdom and perfect in beauty. He was covered with precious stones — sardius, topaz, diamond, beryl, onyx, jasper, sapphire, turquoise and emerald with gold. No wonder he was called Lucifer, which means "morning star."

Ezekiel tells us Lucifer's heart was lifted up in pride because of his beauty; violence filled him within, and he sinned against God. He wanted to ascend above the throne of God and take the place of God.

But God dealt with him right on the spot. His beauty and his light became darkness. His wisdom became corrupted, and he was filled with violence. He became a horror.

A Foe Before Time

The Bible reveals the nature and character of Satan. He has an interest in music, and he is filled with violence. His wisdom is corrupted, which means he does not understand everything and he is indeed confused. He causes many problems on earth as he makes the earth tremble and shakes kingdoms. He has made the world as a wilderness and has destroyed its cities. He refuses to release his captives.

Ezekiel 28 reveals an important truth about Satan. God said to Satan, "I cast you to the ground [earth]" (v. 17) and "I turned you to ashes upon the earth" (v. 18).

The fall of Satan from heaven to the earth must have happened sometime before the creation of man. When? Nobody knows.

The word that Ezekiel uses for *earth* in the above verses is the Hebrew word *erets* which is also used in Genesis 1:1.[1] This means that the earth existed during the fall of Satan, for earth was where God cast him.

In Genesis 1:1 we read, "In the beginning God created the heavens and the earth." When in the beginning? How far back before the creation of man did God make the earth? From biblical chronology we can calculate about six thousand years since the birth of the first Adam. But scientists and archaeologists calculate the earth to be many millions of years old.

Some scholars believe there is a gap in time between the first verse of Genesis and the second verse. The first verse talks about the creation of the earth; the second verse speaks of earth being without form and void. The gap theory speculates that a major catastrophe occurred on earth between these verses.

I don't intend to attempt to prove without a doubt that this theory is actual fact. I am aware that it is an argument from silence — that its validity or its error cannot be proven from recorded Scripture. But without trying to stir up any controversy, let me explain why I think this could make sense.

We know that the animal life that exists today was also in existence before the flood. However, scientists have discovered the bones and fossils of giant dinosaurs. Where did they come from? They didn't exist at the time of the flood because they would have been saved on the ark and therefore some of them would have survived until today.

Another strong point is the portrayal that Isaiah gives us of the earth which differs from Genesis 1:2. It states that God did not create the earth in vain (void, empty).

> For thus says the Lord,
> Who created the heavens,
> Who is God,
> Who formed the earth and made it,
> Who has established it,
> Who did not create it in vain,
> Who formed it to be inhabited:
> I am the Lord, and there is no other (Is. 45:18).

In this verse, the word translated *vain* in Hebrew is *tohuw*, which means "confusion, empty place, without form, waste, vain, vanity or a worthless thing."[2] This verse in Isaiah says God did *not* create the earth in vain, which seems to contradict Genesis 1:2. There must be an explanation why one verse says God did not create the earth in vain and void, while the other verse says that the earth was without form, in vain and void.

I believe there is no contradiction between these descriptions of Genesis and Isaiah. Isaiah portrays the earth when it was created. Genesis, however, describes the condition of the earth before the creation of man. In my opinion, these verses support the theory of a time gap between verses one and two. In other words, something happened to the earth between Genesis 1:1 and Genesis 1:2 which changed the description of the earth from that given in Isaiah 45:18 to that given in Genesis 1:2.

I believe the event of Satan being cast down to the earth recorded in Ezekiel is the catastrophe which caused the earth to change form, becoming a void, waste place. This occurred at some unknown time before man was created.

Earth became filled with Satan's dark presence. It became a wasteland, a wilderness. As Genesis 1:2 states: "The earth was without form, and void; and darkness was on the face of the deep." The word translated *darkness* in Hebrew is *choshek*, meaning "misery, destruction, death, ignorance, sorrow, wickedness."[3]

God did not create the earth filled with sorrow, destruction, death and wickedness. No, God is a good God, and whatever He creates is good. Darkness, death and destruction are the very nature of Satan. He is called the wicked one (Matt. 13:19), murderer (John 8:44), ruler of darkness (Eph. 6:12), him that had the power of death (Heb. 2:14), *Abaddon*[4] (Destroyer, the angel who reigns over the abyss, Rev. 9:11).

Man's Role on Earth

I have asked the Lord why He created man and put him to dwell in the place where Satan was cast down. There are millions of other planets that God could have made habitable for us! Why earth? I do not know if my answer is from the Lord, but I have a feeling that God put us on earth to rule over Satan and his demonic forces.

Adam was the chief in the garden of Eden. He was the ruler and caretaker. He was set in the garden to cultivate, keep and protect it: "Then the Lord God took the man and put him in the garden of Eden to tend and keep it" (Gen. 2:15).

Note the sort of authority God gave him:

> And God blessed them [Adam and Eve] and God said to them, "Be fruitful and multiply, and fill the earth and subdue it; and have dominion over the fish of the sea, over the birds of the air, and over every living thing that moves on the earth" (Gen. 1:28).

To subdue the earth is to gain dominion over it; to master, control, conquer, overcome and vanquish it. The Hebrew word for *subdue* is *kabash,* which means "to tread down, conquer, subjugate, bring into bondage, keep under, bring into subjection."[5]

Was the earth unconquered, untamed and uncontrolled? What was it that God wanted Adam to conquer, to keep under and to bring into subjection? You see, there was something for Adam to overcome and subdue! God told Adam to have dominion over everything that moves on the earth (v. 28). The word translated *dominion*, or *radah* in Hebrew, means "to prevail against, to reign and to rule over."[6]

Adam had been commanded to subdue and rule over

every creeping thing that creeps on the earth. The Bible says that Satan appeared to Eve in the form of a serpent, which means he crept on the ground. Satan was one of those creeping things. God wanted Adam and Eve to prevail against, to reign and rule over Satan. They were supposed to tread him down and overcome his temptations.

But Adam disobeyed God and did not subdue and rule over Satan. Though he had the authority to stamp on that serpent's head and cast him out of the garden, he didn't do it!

Sin is not only doing what God forbids you to do, but also not doing what God wants you to do. Adam was not only guilty of the sin of eating the forbidden fruit, but he also sinned by not taking dominion over Satan.

Adam had the authority. He shouldn't have let that old serpent crawl in his garden to begin with. That garden belonged to Adam and his family. The earth belonged to him. The Bible says, "The heaven, even the heavens, are the Lord's; but the earth He has given to the children of men" (Ps. 115:16).

Man lost his authority and rulership when he sinned. He fell from a kingly position to a place of slavery. He fell from life to death, from health to infirmity, from light to darkness and from joy and peace to a life of suffering and pain. What a fall!

Man lost his territory, position, authority and dominion. He sold his rulership to sin and Satan. He became a slave of sin, bound by Satan. Satan became the ruler and god of this world. "Whose minds the god of this age has blinded, who do not believe, lest the light of the gospel of the glory of Christ, who is the image of God, should shine on them" (2 Cor. 4:4).

This is the sad story of sin and its awful consequences. But the story does not end here. Thanks be to God! God sent His Son and redeemed mankind from sin, its law and its punishment.

> But the free gift is not like the offense. For if by the one man's offense many died, much more the grace of God and the gift by the grace of the one Man, Jesus Christ, abounded to many.
>
> And the gift is not like that which came through the one who sinned. For the judgment which came from one offense resulted in condemnation, but the free gift which came from many offenses resulted in justification.
>
> For if by the one man's offense death reigned through the one, much more those who receive abundance of grace and of the gift of righteousness will reign in life through the One, Jesus Christ.
>
> Therefore, as through one man's offense judgment came to all men, resulting in condemnation, even so through one Man's righteous act the free gift came to all men, resulting in justification of life. For as by one man's disobedience many were made sinners, so also by one Man's obedience many will be made righteous (Rom. 5:15-19).

Thus, through Adam's disobedience death reigned over us, but through the second Adam, Christ Jesus, we reign over death and its dominion. In other words, Adam brought us down, but Jesus lifted us up again. Hallelujah! Isn't this good news? Jesus gave us back the dominion again over sin in this life, over Satan and all the forces of the enemy.

> Behold, I give you the authority to trample on serpents and scorpions, and over all the power of the enemy, and nothing shall by any means hurt you (Luke 10:19).

Now that we are back in our God-given position, there are areas which we must conquer, territories which we must take back from the enemy. We have to take back that which belongs to God.

FOURTEEN

REVIVAL IN THE MUSLIM WORLD

THERE IS A POWERFUL PROMISE in the Bible for the salvation of the children of Ishmael. Isaiah declares:

> Let the wilderness and its cities lift up their voice,
> The villages that Kedar inhabits...Let them give
> glory to the Lord (Is. 42:11-12).

> All the flocks of Kedar shall be gathered together
> to you, the rams of Nebaioth shall minister to
> you;
> They shall ascend with acceptance on my altar,
> And I will glorify the house of My glory (60:7).

Ishmael was Abraham's son by Hagar. The Arabs claim Abraham as their father through Ishmael, their ancestor. Ishmael had twelve sons, among whom were Nebaioth and Kadar. Thus, these promises in Isaiah are for the Arabian people, the majority of whom are Muslims.

There is a mighty move of God today in the Muslim world, a powerful wave of revival and awakening. Many Muslims in the Middle East, Africa, Asia, Europe and America are turning to Christ. Through our crusades alone we have seen thousands upon thousands of Muslims come to Christ in Europe, Africa and Central Asia. God is opening supernatural doors of opportunity for the mass conversion of many Muslims throughout the world.

Disillusioned With Islam

God is allowing massive confusion in the political arena of many Islamic states. Many governments of the Islamic countries in the Middle East and North Africa are oppressive and antidemocratic regimes. Countries like Iran, Iraq, Turkey, Afghanistan, Libya, Algeria, Saudi Arabia and Kuwait are examples. Throughout these countries millions of people are persecuted, imprisoned, tortured and murdered by the secret government police.

Men like Saddam Hussein, Khomeini, Ghadafi, Idi Amin and the Mojahedin of Afghanistan are known for their brutality and their merciless reign over their own people. As a result, many of these people are disillusioned with their leaders and with their God, Allah.

The Islamic revolution of Khomeini brought an uprising of Islamic fanaticism. It also caused a counter reaction among many secular Muslims. Once they experienced the reality of true Islam, secular Muslims who used to be partially protective of the Islamic faith became hateful of Islamic laws and Shari'a. I even know of people who used to be strong Muslim believers but who became hateful towards Islam after only a few years of the reign of the Islamic regime.

History became present reality through the Islamic revolution. Khomeini ushered in the misery and the darkness of seventh-century Arabia to a modern society. This resulted in the migration and flight of several million Iranians to other countries around the world. Many of them had lost their loved ones, their belongings and their identities. Disappointed in Islam and religion, confused and hopeless, they left Iran to start a new life in other parts of the world.

Iranians are not the only group of Muslim immigrants leaving their homeland searching for a meaningful life in the West. There are millions of Afghanis, Kurds, Arabs, Pakistanis, Indians and others scattered throughout Europe, North America and South America. Many of them are now searching for the truth.

The following are testimonies of several former Muslims who became disillusioned with Islam. They heard the message of the gospel, and they responded. Today hundreds of thousands of people wait to hear the same message of hope as Kaveh, Christopher, Tallat and Faheemah. They are waiting for *you* to tell them who Jesus is and what He has done for them.

An Evangelist From Pakistan — Christopher
(written by Maria Waxin, a Swedish columnist)

Christopher was born and raised in a well-to-do family in Pakistan. Christopher's father was a sayyid (direct descendant of Muhammad) Muslim who was highly respected by the people around him. When Christopher was eight years old, his parents were divorced. Christopher's father remarried a woman who did not like Christopher. The rest of his childhood consisted of hate and abuse.

When he was thirteen, he decided to leave home to enroll in an air force military school. But in the military school hate continued to control his life. He was indoctrinated to hate Indians, Jews and Christians. His dream was to kill these people.

When Christopher was seventeen, the war between India and Pakistan broke out, and he saw the chance for his dream to come true. He realized that he hadn't become a perfect man through his zealous practices of Islam. Even with all his fasting and prayers, he could not get rid of his sin consciousness. He was certain that he would not go to heaven if he should die unless he became a martyr.

Christopher was sent to the front line, yet he was not hurt; nor did he die. He returned to the military school, confused and disappointed. Now, not only was he bitter and disappointed in life and in his family, he was also disappointed in Allah who had not let him die and go to heaven.

He lost his faith in everything. Realizing that he didn't even fit in at the military school, he left.

Here Christopher continues to tell his story:

> I tried several different jobs but constantly had the feeling that I was different and out of it. So it didn't take long before I returned to the military school, this time as a reserve officer trainee. But when I graduated from the training, I still felt confused and depressed. So I decided to go to sea. I was taken in a commercial ship going to Lahore, Pakistan. If I couldn't die in the war, I could at least run away from life to the sea, I thought.
>
> One day, when I was in Lahore to do some shopping, I saw a big white man who looked unusually happy. He smiled at everyone, and I was drawn to him. I approached him and asked him who he was. He explained that he was a Christian and that he served Jesus. Then he said

something that shocked me: "Jesus can set you free."

To me, Jesus was a dead prophet, but this man spoke of Him as though He were alive. Something grabbed my heart when I heard about Jesus, and there in the street I decided to give this living Jesus a chance. I prayed very quickly, "Jesus come in my heart, and set me free." When I did, I felt that something happened on the inside of me.

When Christopher told his best friend that he had accepted Jesus in his heart, his friend became very nervous. His friend wrote to Christopher's father and warned him. Before the letter reached Christopher's father, Christopher met some young Christians who were reading the Bible. He had never heard the Word of God before.

"If anyone would come after me, he must deny himself and take up his cross and follow me" (Mark 8:34, NIV). When Christopher heard these words, he knew that it was the call of God to follow Jesus in this way every day.

Immediately he followed the young Christians, passing out tracts and witnessing. He felt that was what God wanted him to continue to do — witness for Jesus to others everyday. Christopher explains, "I was so happy. I had received a totally new life. Finally, I had received something to live for."

By now, his father had found out about his son's conversion. His father, a major, a general and an officer came to talk some sense into him. They said that it was OK if he was drunk or used drugs, but becoming a Christian was the worst thing he could do. It was a shame and scandal for the whole family.

Christopher was taken to a mental hospital where he was totally sedated and observed by armed guards. He had smuggled a New Testament into the hospital in his underpants, and he was able to read a few verses before they drugged him. In spite of being drugged, he was able to witness to a patient and a nurse. They both accepted Jesus. When this became known, they threw him out of the hospital, and his father put him under arrest in his house.

Their house was a big villa with high walls around it, making it difficult to escape. But Christopher was able to sneak out, and with a few pennies in his pocket he took the bus to meet his Christian friends. Even though he was being sought both by the police and the military, he still went out to witness to others about Jesus. Often, there was a riot when people found out that he preached about Jesus.

Eventually, the police were able to find him and put him in jail. After a few months in prison, he was set free. He was then declared under age; this allowed them to confiscate his passport and consequently, he lost his right to get a job.

Once again he became a slave to his dad, forbidden to read his Bible. Once when a Bible was found in Christopher's mattress, the police threatened to arrest him again. He explained, "My father sometimes threatened and sometimes enticed. He was very rich, and he offered to start a business for me or get me a wife. But I just said, 'No, I want to follow Jesus.' Then he threatened to behead me, which according to Islam, a father has a right to do if the child converts to Christ."

With this threat, Christopher realized that it was time to flee. With the help of a Christian family, a Pakistani major and an Iranian diplomat, he was able to get a passport, some money and help to cross the border without lying. With God's help he was able to go to Sweden, where he joined a Bible school and learned more about God's Word.

After Bible school he just wanted to go out and preach. But God told him that he needed to learn something first. All his life Christopher had been taken care of by servants and now, God said that he should learn humility before he would be allowed to preach the way he wanted.

Christopher took a simple job as a cleaner and started to knock on doors to witness. Eventually God opened the door for him to travel and preach the gospel. It all started with sending aid to Poland, where he went and taught a Bible study group. People were healed in those small gatherings. The news spread, and he was called to a home to pray for a paralyzed man who had broken his back. God healed the man, and he got up and jumped and ran.

Since then Christopher has traveled around the world and preached the gospel to masses of people. God has acknowledged His Word with many signs and wonders, and hundreds of thousands of people have been saved and healed.

Christopher concludes:

> Once, when I had preached to a big crowd of people, I saw how God healed many lame and paralyzed people, and I was broken. People were rejoicing, but I went down from the platform, stood behind a fence and cried. I was reminded of who I was and from where I had come.
>
> I said to God, 'I want to die, for no one has seen so much of Your glory and lived.' Then God said that I should go back because He had greater things planned for me.
>
> Imagine the kind of life that Jesus has given me. I am a whole new person with a wonderful future with Jesus. When my father and my stepmother met me after many years, they saw how changed I was. When I was a Muslim, many times I tried to change myself, but I never saw any difference despite how I prayed and fasted. But one meeting with Jesus changed my life.

181

Jesus has the power to change a person's life. He says He will take away our stony hearts and give us new hearts. This is the greatest miracle that can ever happen to someone, and this is what has happened to me.

A Doctor From Iran — by Kaveh

I was born in Iran. From very early on, I had a desire to know God. I remember once when I was about four years old asking my father where God lived, but he couldn't give me an answer. He said that when I started school, my teachers might be able to tell me more about God.

I started school and was taught about Islam, but nobody was able to answer my question. I started praying five times a day as Islam told me I was supposed to in order to please God. I lived in Iran for fourteen years, but during all this time I didn't meet or hear of anybody who truly knew God. Lots of people mentioned Him and talked about Him, but even at my age I could clearly see that God was not a reality in their lives.

Not once did I hear somebody tell me that God had talked to them or that they could pray and have confidence that God had heard and would answer their prayer. There were lots of hopes and *Ensha-Allah's* ("If God wills") that God would hear, but nobody demonstrated the security that only a deep relationship with God can offer.

I moved to Sweden when I was fifteen years old, all the time yearning to know God. Then at age twenty-one I was confronted with Christianity. The Bible told me that God had a deep desire to have a relationship with me! It also said that only my sins stood in my way, but that through believing in Jesus Christ all of my sins would be completely forgiven so that I could enter into a relationship with God. I didn't have to do anything, simply believe that Jesus Christ, by dying on the cross, had paid the full price to free me from my sins; that God had raised Him from the dead as a certain proof of this fact; that God did not count my sins against me; and that I was made completely pure and holy before His eyes — all because of what Jesus Christ had done for me.

This news was too good, too precious and too wonderful not to be taken seriously. I simply believed and asked Jesus Christ into my heart.

Since that day I have entered a relationship with God that deepens daily. I hear God talk to my heart almost daily. I pray, and He hears and answers. Today, I can say that I know God. I know that He loves me. I know His only desire is to bless me and draw me closer to Himself. I know that He is not judgmental, but merciful and gracious. I know that He desires the best for me and for every human being, and I know beyond a shadow of doubt that the only way to Him is Jesus Christ. Jesus said, "I am the way, the truth and the life. No one comes to the Father except through Me" (John 14:6).

I'm a doctor, and I meet many people every day. To this day I've never seen anybody who knows God and has a relationship with Him who hasn't gone through Christ to enter into that holy place. Jesus is the only door into the presence of God — there is no other way.

Paying the Price in Guyana — by Tallat

My name is Tallat Muhammad, and I was born in Guyana, South America, which was formerly a British colony. Guyana is located in the northernmost part of South America and is bordered by Venezuela on the west, Brazil on the south, Surinam on the east and the Atlantic Ocean on the north.

My mother died at the age of twenty-six, two weeks after I was born. I was the last of four children. My father was an alcoholic, and on the day of my mother's funeral he thought I was near death. He wrapped me in cloth and left me on a garbage heap to be burned later in the backyard.

During the funeral my mother's sister came to ask my father where the baby was. He told her I was dead, and he had put me in the backyard. She went back to find me and noticed that there was still a small movement in the wrapped cloth. Realizing that I was still alive, she picked me up and showed me to my father, then asked if she could take me. It didn't seem to matter to him what she did with me, so she took me in and raised me as her own child.

I was very sick, spending most of my first seven to eight years in the hospital. During this period I was never told I had a father or any brothers and sisters, or even that I was adopted. I actually never met my father until I was about seventeen years old. When I did meet him, he blamed me for the death of my mother, which I couldn't understand, nor do I to this date.

Since my aunt (whom I call mother) was Muslim, I was raised and trained to follow the teachings of the Koran. I can remember as a little boy growing up in that environment. My mother and other relatives would go on month-long fasts during the month of Ramadan (during this time we would eat before dawn, then again after sunset). There were many other aspects of Islam that became part of my life, and I became a very dedicated Muslim, adhering to the teachings of Islam.

As I think back, I remember that when I was about seven or eight years old, I visited with a neighbor who told me that Jesus loved me. It was the first time that I had heard the name of Jesus. I lived in a village where almost everyone was Muslim. Not understanding what this person meant, I was curious to find out who this Jesus really was. I asked her to tell me more about this Jesus, and she said that if I came back another day, she would tell me more.

I remember going home and telling my mother about this Jesus who loved me. She then commanded me never to visit that neighbor again, that Jesus was not for us. She told me that Jesus was for the black people and the white people; that we were followers of Muhammad the prophet; that we were called Muslims; and that we worship one God.

I was then sent to Islamic school where I was taught to read the Koran and to study Arabic. I attended this school for a number of years and became very obedient to the teachings of the Koran. During this time I would attend the mosque (which was our place of worship) almost every day to offer prayers. For me Islam was the only religion in the world that was right, and I was proud to be a Muslim.

But as I grew older and began to think about the purpose of my life, I found I had none. I had many questions but not very many answers. Some people tried to answer my questions, but they left me more confused than before I asked. This confusion led to a deep depression in my life for a number of years.

As I saw it, my very existence was purposeless. I did not know where I came from or where I was going, so my conclusion was that life was not worth living.

The further I went into Islam, the more fear became a part of my thought life. Many nights I would be haunted with the words, "Soon you will die, and it will all be over."

As I looked at the lives of the Muslims around me, I saw that their lives didn't line up with what they were teaching. Something was missing. I had religion but no peace, no joy and certainly no love for myself or anyone else. So I tried to produce my own joy and satisfaction by turning to drugs and alcohol. I soon found out that these did not bring me any closer to what I was searching for.

About this time in my life someone invited me to a Christian church. I didn't go because of two reasons: First, I was Muslim, and second, some nights before, I had thrown rocks onto the roof of this church during one of their meetings.

Not long after the invitation to come to that particular church, I was home one evening and was drunk when I heard a voice as clear as if someone were standing beside me talking. After checking and finding that I was home alone, I thought I was going crazy and hearing voices, but I shrugged it off as being nothing.

Then I heard this voice again saying the same thing, although I still did not respond. I later understood that this was God speaking by His Spirit to me. He was basically directing me to go to that church I had thrown rocks on before. I did not understand this, but I could not resist God because He had a plan for my life. I was to go to this church where I would hear about His Son, Jesus.

After hearing the voice the third time, I did go to this church that night. But when I got there I was afraid to go in right away, wondering how they would respond to me, especially considering how badly I had acted towards them. When I did go in, I sat in the back and eventually, because of all the alcohol and drugs, fell asleep.

When I awoke, the meeting had finished, and some of the people came up to me. What I remember distinctly was that they seemed to care about me when they talked to me. This was a feeling that I had never really experienced before. Their loving response to me drew me to come back. I continued coming back for some months but only at night for fear that other Muslim people would see me. The more I attended and heard of Jesus, the more I began to see purpose in life. I then received Jesus as my Lord and personal Savior.

My relatives gave me about two weeks before this would wear off. They then extended it to two months. Then they gradually began to separate themselves from me.

I remember visiting my father in a bar. Two of my brothers also came into the bar. My father's friends asked him who we were. He introduced my two brothers as his sons, but when he came to me, he didn't say anything. It was at this point that I realized living for Jesus would cost me something, and I was prepared to pay whatever it would cost me.

Today after many years of serving the Lord, I have never regretted the decision to be a follower of Jesus. Each day is more exciting than ever.

Even my relatives are becoming interested; some even ask me to pray for them because they have seen a difference in my life and they know how God has really kept me. Some of them tell me how lucky I am. But they don't understand it's not luck. You see, Jesus has power to save as well as power to keep. I give God all the praise for choosing me out of religion into a relationship with Him through His Son, Jesus.

A Convert From the Nation of Islam — by Faheemah Sharrieff

I was born and raised a Baptist. I had heard the name of Jesus in the church as a child, but I knew nothing about this Jesus.

In July 1963 I became a follower of Elijah Mohammad and the Nation of Islam. I didn't know much about the Nation of Islam. But I was attracted to the way their women dressed and how they were treated with so much respect in public. I was fascinated because you always knew a Muslim woman when you saw her. She wore white gannets — all white. The men also wore clean suits and ties; the children, too.

Inside the temple, which is the meeting place, we were taught separation from the white man because he is the devil. Also, we were taught very high self-esteem, unity, militancy, discipline, sewing, cooking, rearing of children and so on.

After the conversion, I could not stay disciplined. I became very disobedient to the laws, such as no smoking and no drinking. I knew certain things were wrong, but I didn't know sin or what sin was. I became a big, confused mess. My whole life was disarranged and confused.

I started using drugs, drinking alcohol and taking pills behind closed doors. I left the temple for a year or so, then came back. I practiced Islam for twenty-five years, praying five times a day and using drugs. Many times I wanted to stop using drugs but could not.

One day in August 1988 I went to the doctor's office to renew a drug prescription. The doctor's nurse happened to be a woman whom I had baby-sat many years ago. I said, "Hello, how are you?" She said to me, "I am blessed of the Lord."

Never before had I heard such words, and some envy sparked within me. I told her how I was tired of living, and she told me she knew a place where there was no sickness or crying. I did not even know where she was talking about. She invited me out, and I went with her, not knowing she was taking me to church.

I accepted the Lord Jesus that night, August 8, 1988. Because of the Lord Jesus Christ redeeming my life from destruction and healing me of all my sickness, I am drug-free and alcohol-free. The Lord Jesus Christ has forgiven me of all my sins and filled me with the most precious gift of the Holy Spirit. I now live a blessed life, full of love, joy, peace, patience, kindness, goodness, faithfulness, gentleness and self-control.

I would like to share this wonderful Lord and Savior Jesus Christ with you. I pray that the Lord will bless you.

Proclaim Their Freedom

Now that you have read the stories of four Muslims set

free by the power of God, you can understand my passion for reaching these people. You understand the spirit of Islam that has them under its dark control. Remember the following facts about Islam.

- Islam is one of Satan's strategies for hindering the kingdom of God.

- Islam denies the deity, death and resurrection of Jesus.

- Islam produces a religious spirit in its followers that results in bloodshed and violence.

- Islam does not offer forgiveness for sins, assurance of eternal life or fellowship with God.

- The holy book of Islam, the Koran, directly contradicts the Bible.

- Islam controls its followers through fear.

- The number of Muslims living in the West is rising as many are fleeing their native lands.

- The Nation of Islam attracts African American converts in the United States by giving people a sense of self-worth and empowerment.

- Muslims depend on good works to give them an opportunity to have eternal life.

- Although every Muslim reveres the Koran, many are unable to read or understand it.

Knowing these things will impact the way you lead a Muslim to salvation. Following are some of the principles I discussed in this book, having learned them through fifteen years of witnessing to Muslims.

- Precede your efforts with prayer and intercession.

- In one-on-one witnessing, concentrate on showing them the love of God.

- Demonstrate the power of God through signs and wonders.

- Avoid belittling or arguing about the Koran or Islamic belief.

- Do not compromise the truth of the gospel, but tell it in terms they can understand.

- Be aware that God may choose to speak to a Muslim directly through a dream or vision.

- Rely on the work of the Holy Spirit, which is the most vital part of Muslim evangelism or any evangelism.

- Plant the Word of God in their hearts because it is a seed that will bear fruit.

We, the people of the church, are the only ones who can bring the Muslims out of darkness into light. May God equip and empower us to bring in His harvest. Amen!

NOTES

Chapter 1
The Spirit of Islam

1. George J. Church, "Laying Hands on an Unwanted Guest," *Time*, 12 July 1993, 27.

2. "Sheik, Fourteen Others Indicted in NYC Bombing Plots," *Tulsa World*, 26 August 1993, sec. A3.

3. Daniel Pipes, *In the Path of God* (New York: Basic Books, 1983), 325.

4. Robin Wright, *Sacred Rage: The Wrath of Militant Islam* (New York: Simon and Schuster, 1985), 44-45.

5. Ibid., 21.

6. Ibid., 31.

7. Robert Morey, *The Islamic Invasion* (Eugene, Oreg.: Harvest House Publishers, 1992), 36.

8. Khomeini, Ayatollah, *Islam and Revolution: Writings and Declarations of Imam Khomeini,* trans. Hamid Algar (Berkeley, Calif.: Mizan Press, 1981), 265-66.

9. *Encyclopedia of Religion,* ed. Paul Meagher, Thomas O'Brian, Consuela Aherne (Washington, D.C.: Corpus Publisher, 1979), I:117, quoted in Morey, *Invasion,* 48.

10. E. M. Wherry, *A Comprehensive Commentary on the Quran* (Osnabruck, Germany: Otto Zeller Verlag, 1973), 36, quoted in Morey, *Invasion,* 50.

Chapter 2
Muhammad and the Origin of Islam

The section on the history of Islam was compiled from the

following sources: Matthew S. Gordon, *Islam* (New York: Facts on File, 1991); William Miller, *A Christian Response to Islam* (Phillipsburg, N.J.: P and R Publishing, 1980); Malise Ruthven, *Islam in the World* (New York: Oxford University Press, 1984).

1. Jill Smolowe, "A Voice of Holy War," *Time,* 15 March 1993, 34.

2. "Surprising Facts You Should Know About Islam," *Scholastic Update*, quoted in George Otis, Jr., *The Last of the Giants* (Tarrytown, N.Y.: Chosen Books, 1991), 75.

3. "Islam Growing in U.K.," *The Church Around the World* 18, no. 1 (1987), quoted in Otis, *Giants,* 75.

4. George W. Braswell Jr., "Christianity Encounters Islam: Iran and Beyond," *Missiology, an International Review* 11, no. 2 (April 1983), quoted in Otis, *Giants,* 75.

5. Charles H. Wagner, "Muhammad's Call," *Magazinet*, (Word of Life Publication, Sweden), December 1990, 19.

6. Robert C. Douglas, "A New Star Over London," *World Christian Magazine,* February 1989, quoted in Otis, *Giants,* 75.

7. Christian church leaders informed Harvesters World Outreach of this during the Harvesters' 1992 mission trip to Kenya.

8. Herbert Buchsbaum, "Islam in America," *Scholastic Update,* 22 October 1993, 15.

Chapter 3
Islam and Violence

1. Wright, *Rage,* 99.

2. Ibid., 83-84.

3. Robin Wright, *In the Name of God: The Khomeini Decade* (New York: Simon and Schuster, 1989), 100.

4. Ervand Abrahamian, *The Iranian Mojahedin* (New Haven, Conn.: Yale University Press, 1989), 220.

5. Wright, *Name of God,* 99.

6. Abrahamian, *The Iranian Mojahedin,* 221.

7. Ibid., 223.

8. Ibid., 206.

9. Khomeini, *Islam and Revolution,* 305.

10. Wright, *Rage,* 36.

11. Ibid., 37.

12. Wright, *Name of God,* 87.

13. *Religion and Politics in Iran,* ed. Keddie, Nikki R. (New Haven, Conn.: Yale University Press, 1983), 180-81.

14. Dilip Hiro, *Holy Wars: The Rise of Islamic Fundamentalism* (New York: Routledge, 1989), 63.

15. Wright, *Rage,* 179.

16. Ibid., 180.

17. Smolowe, "Holy War," 31-34.

18. Ibid., 33.

19. Wright, *Rage,* 35.

20. Wright, *Name of God,* 105.

Chapter 4
Islam in America

1. This number varies from six to eight million people due to the fact that in the United States religion is not part of census. The *Yearbook* is produced by United Methodist Publishing. As quoted in Bob Summer, "The Need to Understand Islam," *Publishers Weekly,* 9 May 1994, 31.

2. Herbert Buchsbaum, "Islam in America," *Scholastic Update,* 22 October 1993, 15.

3. This number varies from 1.5 million to 3 million people.

4. Yvonne Yazbeck Haddad and Jane Idleman Smith, *Muslim Communities in North America* (Albany: State University of New York, 1994), 227.

5. Ibid., xix-xx.

6. Carl Ellis, Project Joseph brochure (Chattanooga, Tenn.)

7. Haddad and Smith, *Muslim Communities,* xix-xx.

8. Ibid., 146.

9. Otis, *Giants,* 74.

10. Carl Ellis, Project Joseph brochure.

11. Ibid., 16.

12. Interview with Carl Ellis on 9 May 1995.

13. Andres Tapia, "Churches Wary of Inner-city Islamic Inroads," *Christianity Today,* 10 January 1994, 36.

14. Louis Farrakhan, interview on 18 May 1989 in Haddad and Smith, *Muslim Communities,* 24.

15. Ibid., 25; quoting from *Chicago Daily Defender,* Big Weekend Edition, 3 December 1977.

16. Ibid., 52; quoting from Simeon Booker, *Black Man's America* (Englewood Cliffs, N.J.: Prentice-Hall, 1964), 116-117.

17. Tapia, "Islamic Inroads," 38.

18. Ibid.

19. Buchsbaum, "Islam in America," 18.

20. Tapia, "Islamic Inroads," 37.

21. Jack Rummel, *Malcolm X: Militant Black Leader* (Philadelphia, Pa.: Chelsea House Publisher, 1989), 71.

22. Interview with Faheemah Sharrieff, 30 May 1995.

Chapter 6
The Confusion of the Koran

1. Morey, *Invasion,* 108.

Chapter 7
Bind the Strong Man

1. William Watt, *Muslim-Christian Encounters, Perceptions and...Perceptions* (London and New York: Routledge, 1991), 41.

Chapter 8
Witnessing to Muslims

1. *The New Strong's Exhaustive Concordance of the Bible* (Nashville, Tenn.: Thomas Nelson, 1984), s.v. "comforter."

Chapter 9
Plant the Word of God in Their Hearts

1. Miller, *A Christian Response to Islam*, 114.

Chapter 11
God's Plan for the Nations

1. Kenneth Scott Latourette, *A History of Christianity* (New York: Harper and Row, 1975), 414.
2. Otis, *Giants*, 238.

Chapter 13
Challenging Giants

1. *Strong's*, s.v. "earth."
2. Ibid., s.v. "vain."
3. Ibid., s.v. "darkness."
4. Ibid., s.v. "Abaddon."
5. Ibid., s.v. "subdue."
6. Ibid., s.v. "dominion."

GLOSSARY

ALI: Son-in-law and cousin of the prophet Muhammad; the one whom the Shiites follow.

ALLAH: The God of Islam.

ARABS OR ARABIANS: The nomads of the steppe land of Arabia. The Arabian peninsula was a dwelling place for various tribal and nomadic groups. The first biblical passage which refers to the inhabitants of Arabia is the table of the nations in Genesis 10.

AYATOLLAH: Means "Sign of God." The highest rank of Shiite clerics.

AYISHA: Muhammad's second wife; daughter of Abu Bakr.

BASIJI: Means "the mobilized." A group of people who are voluntarily mobilized to go to the frontline of battle.

BEHESHT: Means "paradise," a place holding pleasure and joy.

CALIPH: The title of Islamic leaders (successors) after Muhammad's death.

FATWAS: Means "religious decrees." *Fatwas* are given by the highest rank of Muslim clerics and are an interpretation of Islamic law.

HADITH: The reported sayings and actions of Muhammad.

HAJJ: Annual pilgrimage to Mecca. One of the five pillars of the Islamic faith. Compulsory for a Muslim once in a lifetime.

HEZBOLLAH: Means "the party of Allah." It is one of the leading political parties in Iran.

HIJRA: Muhammad's migration from Mecca to Medina in 622. This marks the beginning of Islam, and the Muslim calendar starts with this date.

HUSSEIN: Grandson of the prophet Muhammad and son of Ali, martyred in a seventh-century clash with the Umayyad Dynasty at Karbala.

HUSSEIN, SADDAM: President of Iraq since 1979.

IMAM: Pontiff. A highly respected Muslim leader.

IRP: Islamic Republic Party.

JIHAD: Holy war.

KEDAR AND NEBAIOTH: Sons of Ishmael, who is traditionally known to be the father of the Arabs.

KHADIJEH: Muhammad's first wife.

KHOMEINI, RUHOLLAH: Iran's supreme jurisprudent, popularly known as The Imam.

KORAN: The Islamic holy book. (The Arabic spelling would be 'Qur'n', but it is spelled Koran in this book. The Westernized spelling makes it easier to read for English-speakers.)

MUSAWI, HUSSEIN: Leader of Lebanon's Islamic Amal.

PASDAR: Special city police put in place by Khomeini to insure that Islamic laws were kept in the community — no drinking, no music, proper clothing for women.

RASOUL: God's messenger.

SHARI'A: Islamic law.

SHIITES (or, as originally known, SHI'AT ALI): Followers of Ali. The dispute over leadership of the new Islamic world after the prophet's death in the seventh century led to the biggest schism ever within Islam. Shiites believe in Ali as the successor of Muhammad. Compare to Sunni.

SUNNI: Followers of Omar as the successor of Muhammad.

SURA: A chapter of the Koran.

BIBLIOGRAPHY

Abrahamian, Ervand. *The Iranian Mojahedin.* New Haven, Conn.: Yale University Press, 1989.

Ali, Yusuf. *The Holy Koran.* Brentwood, Md.: Amana Corporation, 1983.

Bernard, Lewis. *The Political Language of Islam.* Chicago: The University of Chicago Press, 1988.

Esposito, John L. *The Islamic Threat.* New York: Oxford University Press, 1992.

————. *Voices of Resurgent Islam.* New York: Oxford University Press, 1983.

Gordon, Matthew S. *Islam.* New York: Facts on File, 1991.

Haddah, Yvonne Yazbeck and Jane Idleman Smith, eds. *Muslim Communities in North America.* Albany, N.Y.: State University of New York Press, 1994.

Hiro, Dilip. *Holy Wars: The Rise of Islamic Fundamentalism.* New York: Routledge, 1989.

Husain, Akbar. *The Revolution in Iran.* Vero Beach, Fla.: Rourke Enterprises Inc., 1988.

Keddie, Nikki R., ed. *Religion and Politics in Iran.* New Haven, Conn.: Yale University Press, 1983.

Khomeini, Ayatollah. *Islam and Revolution: Writings and Declarations of Imam Khomeini.* Translated by Hamid Algar. Berkeley, Calif.: Mizan Press, 1981.

Latourette, Kenneth Scott. *A History of Christianity.* New York: Harper and Row, 1975.

Momen, Moojan. *An Introduction to Shi'i Islam: The Hesagard Doctrines of Twelve Shi'ism.* Oxford, England: George Ronald Publishers, 1985.

Morey, Robert. *The Islamic Invasion.* Eugene, Ore.: Harvest House Publishers, 1992.

Mortimer, Edward. *Faith and Power: The Politics of Islam.* New York: Random House, Vintage Books, 1982.

Otis, George, Jr. *The Last of the Giants.* Tarrytown, N.Y.: Chosen Books, 1991.

Pipes, Daniel. *In the Path of God.* New York: Basic Books, 1983.

Poston, Larry. *Islamic Da'wah in the West.* New York: Oxford University Press, 1992.

Rummel, Jack. *Malcolm X: Militant Black Leader.* Philadelphia, Pa.: Chelsea House Publishers, 1989.

Ruthven, Malise. *Islam in the World.* New York: Oxford University Press, 1984.

Watt, William M. *Muslim-Christian Encounters: Perceptions and Perceptions.* New York: Routledge, 1991.

Wright, Robin. *In the Name of God: The Khomeini Decade.* New York: Simon and Schuster, 1989.

————. *Sacred Rage.* New York: Simon and Schuster, 1985.

ABOUT THE AUTHOR

Reza Safa was born into a Muslim family in the Middle East. He became a devout and practicing Shiite, observing the laws and regulations of Islam. He fasted during the month of Ramadan and prayed five times a day.

After his graduation from high school, Reza felt an emptiness nagging him. The search for truth led him to leave his homeland and reside in the West. Reza finally settled as a student in Sweden, where he heard the message of the gospel for the first time in his life. Reading the Bible in his native language and experiencing the love of God through Christian friends, Reza decided to give Jesus a chance. After months of struggle and doubt, he finally gave his life to Jesus.

He soon moved into full-time ministry, traveling to more than forty countries around the world, reaching masses of unreached people through crusades, church plantings and conferences.

Reza with his family is now based in the United States where he conducts his worldwide ministry. A new thrust of his ministry is outreaches to the inner cities of the United States, targeting the lost, the hurting and the needy people.

DOUBLE-DECKER
OF HOPE PROJECT

One of the greatest arms of The Harvesters World Outreach ministry in the United States is the Double-Decker of Hope Project in the inner cities. Through this bus project they reach thousands of people in the inner cities of America.

Outreaches include:

Outreaches in the ghettos and project areas
Outreaches in the Muslim neighborhoods
Feeding and clothing the homeless
Drama
Power team
Christian rap and pop music
Team evangelism, witnessing, preaching
Youth and children ministries

If you are interested in becoming a part of these great outreaches, or if you would like to become a supporter of these outreaches, you may call or write for further information.

The Harvesters World Outreach

For more information about the author's other publications and ministry products, or to order your copy of *Can Your Faith Stand a Trial?,* a handbook written by Reza Safa directly to Muslims, please contact:

The Harvesters World Outreach
P. O. Box 702094
Tulsa, OK 74170
Phone: 918-488-9645

If you enjoyed *Inside Islam,*
here are some other titles from Charisma House and
Creation House Press that we think will minister to you...

Married to Muhammed
W. L. Cati
A Creation House Press Imprint
ISBN: 0-88419-794-8
Retail Price: $10.99

In this eye-opening exposé of the often deceptive tactics
Muslims use to gain converts, W. L. Cati warns women of the
dangers of dating and marrying Islamic men. Through original
Muslim writings and a chilling account of her own fourteen-
year marriage to a Muslim, Cati sheds light on the dark side of
Islam — especially the teachings and practices that keep
women in suffocating bondage.

Taking Our Cities for God
John Dawson
ISBN: 0-88419-764-8
Retail Price: $13.99

This book invites you to take part in a spiritual clean-up program
that will change you and your community forever! *Taking Our
Cities for God* offers a revised and detailed action plan that will
open the heavens and allow God's blessings to flow freely.

The Missions Addiction
David Shibley
ISBN: 0-88419-772-7
Retail Price: $13.99

In these action-packed pages you will discover a global Jesus
generation that is creating discomfort in the church and change
in missions worldwide. God is calling you to become part of a
contagious epidemic of missions-hearted believers who will
bring global fame to His name!

**To pick up a copy of any of these
titles, contact your local Christian
bookstore or order online at
www.charismawarehouse.com**